TECHNOLOGY

and the

FUTURE OF

FUNDRAISING

MAL WARWICK

The Interactive Edition

This is copy number _255_

ALSO BY MAL WARWICK

Available from Strathmoor Press:

› *How to Write Successful Fundraising Letters* (March 1994)

› *999 Tips, Trends and Guidelines for Successful Direct Mail and Telephone Fundraising* (1993)

› *You Don't Always Get What You Ask For: Using Direct Mail Tests to Raise More Money for Your Organization* (1992)

› *Revolution in the Mailbox: How Direct Mail Fundraising Is Changing the Face of American Society — And How Your Organization Can Benefit* (1990)

TECHNOLOGY AND THE FUTURE OF FUNDRAISING

CONTENTS

PREFACE TO THE INTERACTIVE EDITION

TECHNOLOGY AND THE FUTURE OF FUNDRAISING

Fastened inside the cover of this book you'll find a red envelope.

Inside that envelope is a brief questionnaire. Direct mail fundraisers like me call it an "involvement device." Its purpose is to involve *you*, the reader.

I'm hoping you'll complete my questionnaire as soon as you've read this book. Direct response marketer that I am, I'm also enclosing a Business Reply Envelope, so it will be easy for you to return your questionnaire, and it won't cost you another nickel.

If I hear from you in time, I'll do my best to incorporate your views into a new edition of *Technology and the Future of Fundraising*. And I'll recognize your contribution in print.

Here's hoping I'll hear from you soon!

INTRODUCTION

TECHNOLOGY AND THE FUTURE OF FUNDRAISING

....

W hy is fundraising so old-fashioned?

If you're like me, you call toll-free numbers to order goods from Land's End and Hammacher Schlemmer, using your American Express card. So do most of your donors. Yet most of us resist giving gifts via credit card, and Electronic Funds Transfer sounds futuristic — and possibly indecent.

It's hard to find a business anywhere in America that employs more than a few dozen people and isn't networked to the gills with computer hardware, electronic mail and advanced database management systems. But nonprofits of comparable size are unlikely to be similarly equipped. And all too often the 3 x 5-card is still alive and well in their development departments.

Most of what journalists call "emerging technologies" — inter-networking, "multimedia," wireless communications and other such — are widely available today and in productive use by companies all across the United States. Yet even among fundraising's early adopters — for the most part, those of us who practice the craft of direct mail and telephone fundraising — the use of advanced technology is limited.

But all this will change — soon, and profoundly.

Today's state-of-the-art information management tools and techniques will be part of the *everyday work experience* of fundraisers everywhere in North America before the end of the 21st Century's first decade, at the very latest, and we'll feel the impact a whole lot sooner than that. At any rate, that's the proposition I've advanced in this little book. I've written it in hopes that some of my colleagues will be moved to become *less* old-fashioned — to open up to the myriad ways that contemporary developments in telecommunications, video and computer technology can help us be *better fundraisers*.

This book is intended for nonprofit executives and board members, development directors and consultants, in short, for everyone responsible for the financial health of the nonprofit sector. I hope that reading this slender volume will help move you to increase your investment in the new technologies, and in the staff you'll need to make full use of them. Why? Because I believe you have no choice if you want your organization to survive, much less flourish, in the not-too-distant future. The nonprofit sector, no less than American industry, must devote a larger share of its resources to research and development — and I hope your organization will help point the way in that direction.

A word of caution at the outset, however: this is *not* a how-to book. You won't learn what you can do with a CD-ROM drive or which database software to buy. I won't even presume to tell you which technologies are most worthy of your investment in R&D. This book has a different purpose: I've written it in response to all those questions I've been asked over the years — in meetings with clients, in fundraising workshops, after lectures or in chance encounters — about what fundraisers can expect the future to be like.

"What are the *trends*?" I'm constantly asked.

Well, this book is my effort to describe what I think will prove to be most significant trends — *by envisioning the future*.

....

I 've been living in the future since a very early age. My first effort in creative writing, as I recall, was a fifth-grade science fiction adventure about "Bruce Barton, Space Captain." I no longer have a copy, and all I remember of that juvenile tale is a "needle-nosed spaceship" sitting at a spaceport waiting for a trip to ... somewhere. (Nothing creative about that, I'm afraid — but even Isaac Asimov and Arthur C. Clarke had to start somewhere.)

As an adolescent, and for many years afterward, science fiction and science fantasy were staples in my always heavy reading diet. At times, I gorged on the stuff. For a few years in the 1970s, I even wrote SF for what I wryly called a "living." (You needn't bother looking for the evidence of this chapter in my checkered life; you're unlikely to find anything, since I covered my tracks.) Nonetheless, I've maintained my associate membership in the Science Fiction Writers of America ever since.

However, despite appearances and its undeniably quirky and speculative aspects, this book — excepting one brief chapter — is *not* an exercise in science fiction. It's a lot closer to the "trend analysis" of the fast-growing cadre of futurists.

Consistent with my life-long fascination with things as yet unknown, I've been speculating for years about the future of my chosen craft, direct response fundraising. I devour every available news item, magazine article and book I can find on trends in the trade, and contribute my own views from time to time through the trade press. I read a lot of futurist literature and consume vast quantities of magazines and books about computers. Meanwhile, for the past several years I've seized every opportunity to discuss the future of our work with colleagues and peers.

TECHNOLOGY AND THE FUTURE OF FUNDRAISING

∙∙

This little book is partly the fruit of my reading in the trade press and of discussions with other fundraisers about the long-term prospects for our field. Even more of what I've learned and written is based on insights from people who have little or nothing to do with either direct response or fundraising — people such as Mitchell Kapor, Nicholas Negroponte, Alan Kay, Howard Rheingold, Ted Nelson, David Gelerntner and dozens of others whose names are unfamiliar to most of us in the nonprofit sector. In a larger and more personal sense, however, this book is a linear descendent of my childhood fantasy that, if I tried *really hard* I could somehow see longer and farther down the road than anyone else in the whole wide world. In other words, I've had fun putting this book together. I hope you'll have fun with it, too.

T his book consists of five chapters and six "visual interludes" that attempt to convey my impressions about the impact technology will have on fundraising during the next two decades.

Chapter 1, "Technology and the Future of Fundraising," is adapted from a workshop I led in April 1992 at the national conference of the Social Venture Network, a group of several hundred free-thinking executives, entrepreneurs and investors dedicated to promoting social responsibility in the business community and in their own lives. In this chapter, I've examined the broader context in which we ply our craft.

In Chapter 2, "Six Keys to 21st Century Fundraising," I've attempted to pinpoint the characteristics I believe will dominate the fundraising appeals we send in the early decades of the 21st Century. This piece is adapted from a video presentation I first delivered at

TECHNOLOGY AND THE FUTURE OF FUNDRAISING

the 1993 International Conference on Fund Raising in Atlanta, Georgia, sponsored by the National Society of Fund Raising Executives (NSFRE). If you happened to witness that presentation — which I've since repeated in several other cities — you may notice a few changes in my conclusions.

Chapter 3, "Do Fundraisers Dream of Electronic Funds?", is a light-hearted look at the day-to-day experience of attempting to practice a high-touch craft in a high-tech world. Through the technique of scenario-building, familiar to everyone who reads futurist literature, I hope to bring to life some of the abstractions that dominate the earlier chapters in this book. I prepared an earlier version of this piece for distribution at a workshop in January 1992 for the national conference of the American Association of Political Consultants.

"Peering into the Future of Direct Response Fundraising," which appears as Chapter 4, was part of a much longer essay I wrote for an all-day workshop on "The Future of Fundraising" in San Francisco in July 1993. (So is the chart labeled "The Changing World of Direct Response Fundraising" that's included as a visual interlude on page xx.) In this short piece, I took a straightforward look at some of the major implications for the direct response fundraising industry of the technological changes discussed throughout the book.

Chapter 5 is "An Annotated Reading List." I developed this bibliography of 178 books, articles and newspaper stories throughout 1992 and 1993. Earlier versions were handed out in several of the workshops and other presentations noted above. Since then, however, I've substantially expanded the bibliography and completely reorganized it, in hopes of making it more useful for readers who are less enthralled with technology than I.

....

Before and after these five chapters are illustrations and sidebars I've collectively termed visual interludes. Each of the six is an attempt to dramatize the trends addressed in the text or to put the whole subject of the future in perspective.

After all, it's *perspective* that we're all seeking — what the Yale computer maven, David Gelerntner, calls "topview."

Participants in my workshops contributed a lot to the making of this book. So did several other people, especially my assistant, Ina Cooper. Ina coordinated the book's production and the countless details that made it possible, far more ably than I would ever have been able to do — and her tireless efforts to protect my writing time enabled me to meet self-imposed but nonetheless merciless production deadlines. I'm also indebted to Jim Aldigé (Transamerica Marketing Services), James A. Vonderheide (Russ Reid Company), Gene Henderson (Epsilon) and Roger Hiyama (Saturn Corp.) for reviewing the draft manuscript; their comments were both insightful and helpful. The final product is much changed — and greatly improved — because of their contributions.

Stephen Hitchcock made the biggest difference, however — and you, the reader, are the beneficiary. Steve went through my draft copy wielding a ready pen; he left the evidence on nearly every page — and returned the whole marked-up mess with a cover memo that forced me to rethink how I'd organized and framed the material. As a result, this book is different from what it was at first, and far more useful for you, I hope.

....

Throughout this book, I've emphasized direct response fundraising (direct mail and telephone fundraising). I know that field better than any other — but I also believe the natural outcome of the technological convergence so widely noticed today by the popular media is that eventually (but sooner, rather than later) *all* fundraising will involve what we today think of as direct response. What I've written on the pages that follow will explain that assertion — to your satisfaction, I hope.

You'll find out. Just read on.

— Berkeley, California
December 1994

TECHNOLOGY AND THE FUTURE OF FUNDRAISING

The Changing Role of Technology in Our Lives at Work

A meeting is a meeting is a meeting — right? Well, maybe not any longer.

For centuries without number, to hold a business meeting meant simply that, and nothing more. Then, less than one century ago, the telephone dropped into our lives on the job. All of a sudden, there were two options for business meetings: face-to-face — or by phone. Yet telephone meetings were clumsy at best: if you wanted to meet with more than one person at a time, they all had to gather around a speaker-phone on one end or the other or listen in on extensions. Either way, the quality of the sound was generally poor — enough to be annoying.

As recently as fifteen or twenty years ago, sitting down face-to-face or talking one-on-one by phone remained the only two ways for working people to meet (at least for the overwhelming majority of us). In the intervening years, telephone technology has been dramatically upgraded while long-distance costs have plummeted, bringing the conference call within reach for millions of businesspeople.

Meanwhile, the advent of small, affordable computers, Local Area Networks (LANs), electronic mail ("E-mail") and computer bulletin board systems (BBS) have made it possible

FUNCTION	1st Generation	Contemporary	New Wave
Communications	telephone mail	fax E-mail voice-mail	groupware
Training	face-to-face audiocassettes	videocassettes	expert systems virtual reality
Presentations	slides transparencies	software packages	multimedia color laser printers
Writing & formatting text	pencil & paper electric typewriter	word-processor desktop publishing	multimedia
Financial calculations	paper & pencil	spreadsheets	neural networks
Meetings	face-to-face telephone	conference calls E-mail	computer- assisted meetings

TECHNOLOGY AND THE FUTURE OF FUNDRAISING

....

for us to hold meetings electronically. Now, using these simple and readily available technologies, we can exchange news and views simultaneously ("in real time"), at great distances or small. As a result, today many of us are holding meetings by computer that are just as informative, efficient and satisfying as those we held by perching on desks around a speaker-phone or shouting into an mouthpiece! Wonderful, isn't it?

*Wait: this **does** get better.*

Already, using "groupware," it's possible to hold same-time, different-place, computer-mediated meetings — and actually enjoy the experience. Groupware allows people working in different locations to work simultaneously on the same text or graphics; this new class of software is now available on the open market and widely used in some large organizations. (As we go to press, the current iteration of "Notes" from Lotus Development Corp., the most popular of these products, is Version 3.0.) Other big companies maintain special facilities for same-time, same-place meetings where on-site facilitators and souped-up software speed discussion and produce genuine consensus, extracting views from even the quietist person in the room. Within a very few years, both groupware and meeting process management systems will be in wide use — and their capabilities are already starting to merge.

These computer-assisted meetings may yield a qualitatively different — and better — experience than the face-to-face or telephone meetings of the past. Many people who've used these systems report they accomplish more. Why? There are two reasons, I believe: (1) Software systems such as groupware lend structure to the meeting process. (2) The technology compensates for many of the human quirks and foibles that get in the way when we just talk together.

These new technologies that are intruding in our meeting rooms are just one of a great many new products, forms and procedures that will collectively make our lives at work dramatically different from what we experience today. The table on page 17 gives a forty-year overview. "First Generation" technologies were widely employed in the 1960s and 1970s when direct response fundraising came to be widely used by nonprofits on both a regional and a national level. Most "Contemporary" technologies were widely used in the 1980s and 1990s. "New Wave" technologies haven't yet gained wide acceptance — but they'll be common in fundraising programs of all types, on a small scale as well as large — within the first decade of the 21st Century.

TECHNOLOGY AND THE FUTURE OF FUNDRAISING

1

A never-ending parade of new information technologies confounds and amazes us.

Day after day, year after year, the new gadgets and gizmos explode into our lives — invading our television screens and the front pages of our newspapers, our stores and consumer catalogs. For most Americans, numbness has long since set in.

But even in the most remote backwaters of the nonprofit world, where fear of change is sometimes confused with ethics, fundraisers can't afford to ignore the newly emerging technologies. Taken singly, the New Age machines spawned by the microprocessor — the video games, the cellular phones, the notebook computers — may be trivial. Taken together, devices like these are changing the shape of our universe, and none of us will escape their impact. Swiftly moving technological currents are now swirling about virtually every aspect of our lives in America on the verge of the 21st Century. Soon, much of what we take for granted in our society will be profoundly changed:

› the ways our goods are manufactured and distributed, and basic services defined and delivered;

› the ways we work and play and shop;

› the ways we organize and operate both public and private institutions, conduct the business of cities and states and choose our society's leaders;

› the ways we obtain and analyze information about the world around us;

TECHNOLOGY AND THE FUTURE OF FUNDRAISING

⋯⋯⋯⋯⋯⋯⋯⋯⋯⋯⋯⋯⋯⋯⋯⋯⋯⋯⋯⋯⋯⋯⋯⋯⋯⋯

›   even the ways we think about our lives and our futures: our hopes, our fears, our values.

With dramatic new opportunities — and new limitations — all about us, no individual can expect to live a fulfilling life in the new world now emerging without learning new ways to think, to learn and to act. And no organization will flourish without making profound adjustments — redefining its structure, its mode of operations, its very purpose.

In the light of these earth-shifting developments, how can the craft of fundraising and the charities it serves be anything but profoundly changed?

To help illuminate the future of fundraising, I'll focus on the changes I foresee in the field I know best: direct mail fundraising. Direct mail is typically seen as just one of a great many fundraising tools and techniques — though it's the *principal* means by which many of the nation's largest and most influential nonprofit organizations have been launched and grown to prominence. Direct mail — now frequently termed "direct response," to embrace its twin, telephone fundraising — is the largest single source of new donors to charity in the U.S. And direct response techniques are playing an increasingly prominent role in securing major gifts as well as bequests and other planned gifts. The methodologies of direct response have also been successfully put to work in such disparate fundraising activities as capital campaigns, employee giving programs and special events, and they're a mainstay of the annual funds and membership programs which are bread and butter to thousands of charities.

In other words, I'm convinced the future of fundraising *is* the future of direct response. The influence of direct mail and telephone fundraising techniques can only continue to broaden over the years. Why? For three reasons:

The nation's leading charities keep growing larger and more diverse, forcing development staff to pick and choose their direct donor contacts with ever greater care and rely on indirect means to handle the rest.

Americans move from city to city every five years on the average, so that every year more and more of our donors are physically out of reach. Direct, face-to-face contact becomes more difficult with every passing year.

Direct response itself is becoming ever more flexible and better attuned to the quirks and foibles of donors.

But will fundraising twenty years from now, in the year 2014, be simply the same old business — some new variation on Publishers Clearing House sweepstakes mailings conducted with fancy new gadgets and gizmos?

Absolutely not!

The business of direct mail fundraising is changing in genuinely *fundamental* ways under the onslaught of new technologies. Consider what's already happened in direct response in recent decades by taking a look at the changes we've experienced in each of four basic, real-world aspects of our life and work as fundraisers:

1   RELATIONSHIPS

Every good fundraiser knows that the *relationship* between the donor and the charity is what fundraising is all about. (That's true of every form of marketing.) And that relationship is already beginning to change in profound ways, as a result of new capabilities afforded us by emerging, microprocessor-based technologies.

Twenty years ago, most direct mail fundraisers related to the public as members of one or two very broad categories: a given individual was either a *donor* — or not a donor, that is, a *prospect*.

Today, we know a lot more about donors' behavior and preferences than was known twenty years ago. Most of us in the field manage to relate to donors as members of a great many small groups ("segments") that are tightly defined by their previous behavior toward a particular charity. In other words, we don't look at the public nearly so simplistically as we used to. Now we can identify and approach many different types and classes of *prospects*, and an ever greater variety of actual *donors* to any given organization.

Even now, some technically more proficient and better-funded direct mail fundraising programs are beginning to look at donors not as members of groups or segments but ... lo and behold! ... as *individuals*. By harnessing computer power in our database management programs with exotic new printing presses, we already have the capability to address *unique* messages to every donor.

Few organizations can afford all that in 1994. And it's not just the high cost of the fancy hardware that holds back most charities; the larger problem typically lies on the human side, in overworked staff members ill-equipped to plan and learn the necessary technical skills.

But, within fifteen or twenty years at the outside, we won't be able to afford *not* to treat all our donors as individuals. Donors will *expect* it. They simply won't send gifts unless we honor their wishes not to receive unsolicited mail from other charities with whom their names have been exchanged ... or to be solicited only once per year ... or not to be sent the newsletter ... or never to be phoned at dinnertime. In fact, fundraisers had better wake up soon and refine their direct response systems and procedures. We *must* treat our donors like the thinking individuals they are and honor their preferences for respectful treatment; otherwise state charities regulators — or the U.S. Congress — will force us to do so!

2 HOW AND WHERE WE WORK

Those of us who are employed in the Third Sector two decades from now will also relate to our co-workers and employers in dramatically new ways. Our experience of the character of work itself will be different in several significant ways — and this will be true whether we're raising funds for the Nature Conservancy or a local human service agency:

The fortunate few who master the tools of the trade will have immense power at their fingertips: the power to reach millions with minimal physical effort and at modest cost; and the power to control the communications process virtually from conception to delivery, with far less help from others than is necessary now.

Nonetheless, the cost and complexity of the new telecommunications technologies is likely to make the future secure for vendors offering specialized services, which few nonprofit organizations (or businesses) will be able to afford — or to understand. The "user-friendliness" much promised by today's computer merchants will always lag the leading edge of technology — no matter how much the engineers and programmers succeed in refining such innovations as voice recognition, expert systems, neural networks and "object-orientation." (These are among the most promising

....

current efforts to bring technology down to human scale, but like most machine-based technologies the *greater* promise is that they'll only become more complex as time goes on!) So — since it's precisely on the leading edge that competitive advantage is gained — those nonprofits that want to stay ahead of the game will need to "out-source" new technical knowledge. As a result, I believe, consultants like me will be in business for a long time to come.

But *our* work-a-day world will change too, and for the same reasons. Consultants and other vendors of communications services are likely to be grouped either in large, well-capitalized firms or in loose, shifting alliances of small, highly specialized companies and solo practitioners with unique skills to market. The New Age is just too complicated and too competitive for generalists working alone; we'll all need continuing connections to people with arcane knowl-edge — because it's indispensable to set up the systems we depend on, and to keep them working.

The "Renaissance Man" of the 16th Century understood the world he lived in, having mastered several languages and a dozen disciplines; no one, however intelligent or omnivorous in reading habits, can possibly hope to gain a comprehensive understanding of the late 20th Century world, much less all its myriad technologies. Every specialized field has its own language, its own set of rules, its own prevailing world-view, its own customs. Who, today, can succeed as a specialist in a dozen fields at once? No one: there's far too much for any mortal brain to retain. And the sum total of human knowledge continues to increase at a geometric rate.

In some ways, though, our work may become easier and more pleasurable.

Regardless of where we're employed — whether in-house at a large company or nonprofit institution, or in a small, independent consulting firm — we'll be able to pick and choose the hours and physical location of our work. New, mobile technologies are beginning to free us from the constraints of time and space. Within twenty years, wireless communications devices and "telephone numbers" assigned to us as individuals — not to any particular *place* — will enable us to reach others, and be reached (when we wish), regardless of where we happened to have alighted at any given moment. Today's "telecommuting," limited to an adventurous few, will become a way of life for most of tomorrow's specialists.

3   COMMUNICATIONS MEDIA

Nowadays, one of the hottest debates on the business pages of the nation's leading newspapers is over whether the cable TV industry or the telephone companies will prevail in their attempts to control the fiber-optic networks of the future — the means by which, sooner or later, we're all likely to receive most of our information and entertainment. But it doesn't really matter *which* industry wins — or if neither does. (Among other unlikely players, the electric utility companies are now sneaking into the act and may take us all by surprise!) Fiber-optics are on the way, and with them the capability to transmit and receive enormous amounts of data (visual, audio and text) simultaneously.

But the new world of fiber-optics will affect a whole lot more than our range of choices on TV and the bells and whistles in our telephone service. Obviously, there are profound social and political implications, and I'll have something to say about them later in this book. However, the fast-growing Information Superhighway will alter the very character of our daily interaction with the world around

us: our relations with our employers and co-workers, with friends
and family, with educational and financial institutions, with many of
those who sell us goods and services — and with our favorite
charities.

By 2014, much of the infrastructure of daily life in U.S. society
today — mail, telephone, television, newspapers, cable TV, personal
checking accounts, marketing and merchandizing — will have taken
unrecognizable forms. All this, and more, will eventually merge into
a multi-channel communications system that every individual — at
least, everyone who can afford it — will depend on, every moment
of every day. We'll tap into this system to show the doctor how the
swelling went down, to call Aunt Minnie with news of the kids, to
shop for a sweater in just the right color, to keep a line open for news
about Granddad's surgery, to pay the month's bills — and to send
a gift in response to an emergency appeal for earthquake victims.

Now, I don't mean to suggest that the vaunted Information
Superhighway will replace all we hold dear (or at least familiar) within
the next two decades. Just as radio has experienced a rebirth in the
heyday of television, the U.S. Postal Service will still be delivering
billions of letters — by hand. We'll still be reading books — some of
us, anyway. Newspapers will still be on sale in many towns and
cities. Checking accounts will continue to be widely used. The
multi-channel system that represents the merger of today's communications technologies — "the Network," as it may come to be called
— will *gradually* supplant the systems now familiar to us. For
decades, its impact will be additive — evolutionary rather than
revolutionary.

It *will* happen, though. I fully expect that some day soon I'll
be using the mails — what computer jocks call "snail-mail" — to tip
off donors about special multimedia programs available on the

Network that highlight a charity's latest accomplishments. Already, some enterprising nonprofits use the mails for precisely that purpose: to call attention to TV or cable specials.

4   INFORMATION VS. KNOWLEDGE

The Network will give us access to a virtually unlimited store of information — and the power to define and control which information we receive, and when, and in what form.

Today's news ... tonight's entertainment listings in local theaters and "TV" ... the weekend's accumulated telephone messages ... the second draft of the organization's strategic plan, forwarded by the Executive Director ... *and a week's worth of charitable solicitations* — all might come flashing across the wallscreen, or condensed into paper summaries, or timed to appear at appropriate intervals as we prepare dinner or put on a change of clothing. The choice will be ours.

That choice — how we manage the information glut — will mean the difference between information and *knowledge.*

Some day, most of the contents of the Library of Congress will be accessible from every home. So will the output of every news network on the planet. Any day. Any time. That prospect strikes most of us as frightening (and it probably should!) It's intimidating to think about how to cope with what is, effectively, the sum total of human knowledge — in a box. But it's only *information* to you and me, not knowledge, unless it's interesting to us personally — unless it's *useful.* Fortunately, the information management technologies now emerging will afford us the ability to winnow through mountains of useless data and find the information that is of value to us as individuals — to convert information into knowledge.

Take the day's news, for example. Every morning when I'm at home, I read two newspapers; as a slave to habit, I perform a daily ritual, sorting through them to find the news *I* want. First I discard any sections devoted to home, food, travel or sports. Then I scan the headlines of what's left, ignoring most (but not all) the ads and looking for stories on just those topics that interest me: the day's *top* news stories; articles about politics and social policy; business news, especially marketing and advertising; everything I can find about nonprofits and fundraising; anything about technology. On any given weekday, I may find fifty stories that meet my criteria — but actually *read* no more than a dozen.

In the future, I expect this experience to be changed in three ways:

1 My communications system will have the capability to do that sorting for me — to offer up those fifty stories I myself would choose. How? Because I'll tell the system exactly what to look for. (At first, the system may offer me a hundred choices — failing to distinguish between "food markets" and "marketing," for instance — but it'll learn more about my preferences as time goes on.)

2 Among the dozen stories I elect to read, several, perhaps all, will contain lots *more* information than my newspapers now see fit to print: the full text of a correspondent's dispatch from Sarajevo; the entire annual report of a company featured in the news; the IRS Form 990 filed by a charity accused of fraud.

3 Many stories in the news will be multimedia reports, consisting not just of text and two-dimensional graphics but sound and moving images as well (perhaps ultimately holographic three-dimensional images). A story about changing trends in philanthropy might include on-camera interviews with the heads of leading charities, a video extravaganza produced by a foundation as its annual report and a tape of the keynote address at the NSFRE international conference.

Of all the changes in store for us in the next two decades, this enhanced ability to manage information may be the most far-reaching. For now — at long last — we're entering the long-promised Age of Knowledge.

But it's not just us fundraisers who will have these capabilities. Our donors will, too!

With the world literally at their fingertips — and the power to distinguish between what they think is important to know, and what isn't — donors will be able to pick and choose the charities they support from a much broader array of choices. They'll have tools available to find us if our organizations answer the needs that concern *them*. Simply to compete, we'll be forced to make available all the information that donors will need to make intelligent choices.

Today, donors — like all consumers — are befuddled by the competing claims and counterclaims of the charitable marketplace. Twenty years from now, a few thoughtful questions channeled through a personal communicator onto the worldwide information network will uncover a wealth of comparative data about nonprofit organizations and institutions working in any given field ... or in *every* field. Every nonprofit organization will face the same cold-eyed scrutiny. And donors won't just be looking at the nature or the effectiveness of the programs we ask them to support, or the attractiveness of the benefits we offer them: they'll be evaluating *us* to determine how honest, how forthcoming, how credible we are. They'll be able to cut us off in an instant if they learn we're not doing the job we claim or don't honor the values they hold dear.

··

DANGERS AND DILEMMAS

It's naive, even polyannish, to delve into this vast subject of technological change without acknowledging the potentially profound negative social and political consequences. The principal elements of potential trouble appear to lie in the following areas:

› CIVIL LIBERTIES — Direct marketers now typically identify privacy as the overriding issue of their industry in the 1990s, and fundraisers who use the mails are becoming increasingly aware of the issue. With the widening reach of computer networks and the spread of ever more intelligent software that can glean useful information from a welter of previously unreadable data, individual Americans could be prey to new and more invasive forms of abuse by both business and government. If you believe some outspoken members of Congress, nonprofits are part of the problem, too — trafficking in sensitive personal information about their donors, or simply exchanging mailing lists. (I, for one, think there's a big difference between exchanging lists of names and addresses and employing private investigators to dig up dirt on donors!)

› HAVES AND HAVE-NOTS — The cost of new technologies will be a barrier to entry for many poor people, who may as a result be shut off from access to the information we'll all need merely to survive in an information-driven world. But a far more common barrier is likely to be a lack of the skills necessary to obtain and manipulate basic information. Today, "user-friendliness" is no help to someone who doesn't know the first thing about operating a computer; in the future, using a worldwide information network will require a much higher level of education and judgment than merely handling floppy diskettes and pressing keys on a keyboard. Because the use of information requires high-level abstraction and conceptual skills, which are rare in any society, the *majority* of Americans are likely to be excluded from the greatest benefits of the new technologies for decades to come.

› SOCIAL ISOLATION — The near-universal availability of information on virtually every topic imaginable will foster the creation of innumerable latter-day "intentional communities" that are free of many of the constraints of time and geography. Many of us will derive enormous personal satisfaction from such special interest groups. Thousands already participate in "virtual communities" through computer bulletin-board systems under the wing of such on-lone services as CompuServe, America Online, Prodigy, The Well or the sprawling, worldwide hodge-podge of public and private networks called the Internet. But most Americans will shun such opportunities. For many of us today, sitting in front of a computer screen engaged in our pursuits is as isolating as the life of a couch potato, eyes glued to the television screen, oblivious of everything and everyone else. New shapes and forms of community will be needed to sustain the spirit and help individuals find fulfillment in a world of bewildering scope and complexity — and virtually unlimited distractions.

› INSTITUTIONAL STRAIN — Given the cracks in the infrastructure of our society — our schools, our health care delivery system and governments at every level, as well as our roads and bridges — America's basic institutions may be unable to adapt to the epochal changes new technologies are bringing in their wake. The explosive potential of this inherently unstable situation is enormous. Already volatile and increasingly unpredictable, the American electorate could strike back at change, and at the failure of our institutions, in truly terrible ways. More than anything else, I fear the possibility that some new form of fascism will flourish if the worst comes to pass and America's leaders fail to restore the long-term vitality of our economy.

In the face of such deep-seated dangers, how can we turn the new technologies to our advantage — making useful tools of them and not becoming victims to their awesome manipulative potential?

The answer to this question ultimately lies in our attitudes about the nature of society. I believe we'll find an acceptable answer only through a redoubled commitment to basic human rights — a far-sighted understanding that none of us can lead lives of security and self-fulfillment in a society that denies dignity to millions of our fellow citizens.

Innovative Magazines Foreshadow the Future

Increasingly, the printing, production and personalization of direct mail fundraising appeals are merging into a single, on-line process. A path-finding magazine is an early example of where these trends might carry us all twenty years from now. Since 1984, Farm Journal has been produced through a process known as "selective binding and inserting" or "selectronic binding." Both the editorial contents and the advertising matter are selected and printed for each subscriber on the basis of individual interests and needs. Farm Journal has a circulation of just 700,000. The similar-looking copies pictured here represent eight out of more than 5,000 different versions of the February 1993 issue (including 280 distinct editions). Some of these copies are fat, while others are thin — because their contents are different.

Selectronic binding is just one of several ways that publishers are using the power of on-line production systems to address their individual subscribers. Other magazines routinely feature ads — inside — containing the individual's name and address.

For fundraisers, such printing techniques portend a future when we can respond to every donor's individual needs and preferences — in every appeal.

Farm Journal

The Magazine of American Agriculture

FEBRUARY 1993

James Anderson:
**Farm Steward
of the Year**

Crackdown on manure

Crime can be murder on your taxes

Farm Journal

The Magazine of American Agriculture

FEBRUARY 1993

James Anderson:
**Farm Steward
of the Year**

Crackdown on manure

Crime can be murder on your taxes

Farm Journal

The Magazine of American Agriculture

FEBRUARY 1993

James Anderson:
**Farm Steward
of the Year**

Crackdown on manure

Crime can be murder on your taxes

Farm Journal

The Magazine of American Agriculture

FEBRUARY 1993

James Anderson:
**Farm Steward
of the Year**

Crackdown on manure

Crime can be murder on your taxes

Farm Journal

Farm Journal

SIX KEYS TO 21ST CENTURY FUNDRAISING

2

TECHNOLOGY AND THE FUTURE OF FUNDRAISING

I t's impossible to foretell the shape or direction of the future — especially where technology is concerned. But this much I'll predict: the direct response fundraising systems we'll depend on twenty years from now will share the following six characteristics.

› INDIVIDUALIZED. Our appeals will be "individualized." By and large, we won't be dealing with donor file "segments" anymore but with individuals — responding to their unique, personal interests and capabilities. We'll know a lot more about our donors, because we'll ask them for more information through frequent surveys and questionnaires and because our information management systems will be capable of storing much more data than most charities now find practical to retain.

› MULTI-SENSORY. Our appeals will be "multi-sensory," using forms of what today are called "multimedia" technologies. We won't be limited to paper, or to voice communications, or to pre-recorded sounds or video images. A single fundraising appeal might consist of sights, sounds and data, and be delivered, separately or simultaneously, through several communications channels: a wallscreen, perhaps, with full-motion sound and video, or a pocket communicator bearing a simplified, two-dimensional version, or a hardcopy printout a little like what today we call a "fax." Donors will choose which method they prefer, and open it up when and where they wish — suiting the mood or constraints of the moment, or following long-established preferences for one form or another.

› INFORMATION-RICH. Twenty years from now, our appeals will be "information-rich." On-line databases and super-high-speed

TECHNOLOGY AND THE FUTURE OF FUNDRAISING

··

data transmission will permit us to make veritable mountains of information available to every prospect or donor — and the demands of competition will force us to do so. Meanwhile, flexible database management software will permit every prospect and every donor to select precisely those bits of information they want — and not one word or one image more. Just as I program my communications system to pre-select news stories I'm likely to find interesting, donors to my clients will teach their own software "agents" to sift through mountains of information — including newsletters, bulletins, annual reports and special appeals from charities — to pick those that match their own interests or circumstances.

›   REAL-TIME. Within two decades, "real-time" transactions will be common in direct response fundraising. "Real-time" is computer jargon for "right now." For example, by authorizing a gift in the course of an on-line videoconference with her favorite charity, a donor may instantaneously transmit funds from her bank account to the charity — before the conference is even over. The response curves we measure today in weeks and months may be viewed in terms of hours or even minutes twenty years from now.

›   INTERACTIVE. Fundraising thirty years from today will be highly "interactive." Donors will actively participate, not just in selecting the amount and the format of the information they receive, but the role they'll play in the life and work of the charities they support. Today's dedicated donor "hotlines" will become multimedia gateways that offer donors a multitude of new options: to participate in the latter-day equivalent of focus group research, for example, or to share their specialized expertise with program staff, or to integrate what they're

TECHNOLOGY AND THE FUTURE OF FUNDRAISING

learning from us into ongoing educational programs. Both two-way and small-group communications will be an integral part of the process — freeing fundraisers from the constraints of time and geography, and permitting us to develop rich and rewarding relationships with donors we may never actually meet.

> COMMUNAL. The nonprofits that flourish in the fast-moving environment of the 21st Century will be those that provide their supporters with the experience of community. Today's fast-multiplying computer networks, bulletin board systems, local access cable TV, video teleconferencing and E-mail facilities foreshadow the integrated technologies of the 21st Century. Within twenty years, charities will be able to engage thousands of their donors in a profoundly personal and meaningful way — simultaneously, and over great physical distances. Meanwhile, as individuals, many donors will find the nearly instantaneous, broadband communications of the New Age will permit them to turn a shared commitment to a charity's work into personal relationships with many of their fellow donors. Just as users of today's converging technologies are forming "virtual communities," often spanning continents and oceans, donors by the thousands may eventually be able to join with a charity's other constituents — staff, board, clients, alumni — in shared access to the daily experience of the charity's work. How? Through a latter-day equivalent to "personals" ads in the newsletters or public forums on the Network of the future. That experience and the personal relationships that result may enrich daily life in the 21st Century for tens of millions of people.

TECHNOLOGY AND THE FUTURE OF FUNDRAISING

The Changing World of Direct Response Fundraising

The chart on the opposite page depicts the tools and techniques widely (though by no means universally) employed at each of three stages in the evolution of direct response fundraising. Please don't send letters protesting the details. This is an effort to convey the pace and direction of change, not to illustrate the specific characteristics of any aspect of the field.

FUNCTION	1974	1994	2014?
Copywriting & approvals	IBM Selectric & paper	Word-processor, paper, diskette, LAN	Groupware
Design & typesetting	Paste-up, Linotronic, still some lead type	Desktop publishing	High-resolution color, integrated sound & video
Budgeting & projections	Pencil & paper, calculator	Spreadsheet, database management	Expert system, computer modeling
Targeting	ZIP code	ZIP+4, psychographics, geodemographics	ZIP+4+4, neural network, expert system
List selection	Data cards, merge-purge	Database management, merge-purge	Neural network
Database maintenance	Mainframe computer, magnetic tape	Microcomputer, LAN, hard disk drive	Computer model, CD-ROM, WAN
Segmentation	Prospects vs. donors	Recency, frequency & gift amount	Multivariate analysis
Printing	Web press, sheet-fed	Laser printer, on-line web press	On-line web, selective binding & inserting
Personalization	Cheshire label, match-fill	Cheshire label, laser printer, on-line web press	Selective binding & inserting, audio & video
Lettershop	Cheshire label, multi-station inserter	High-speed inserter	On line
Message delivery	Mail, outbound telephone	Mail, outbound & inbound phone, video & audio	On-line multimedia, IVR, electronic retrieval
Donor involvement	Reply device, premium	Reply device, 800-number	On-line conferencing
Caging & cashiering	Manual processing, batch processing	On-line database management	Electronic Funds Transfer

DO FUNDRAISERS DREAM OF ELECTRONIC FUNDS?

3

TECHNOLOGY AND THE FUTURE OF FUNDRAISING

Y ou're probably wondering how all these whiz-bang new technologies will change the daily experience of our life as fundraisers. I wonder, too.

For starters, word-processing software and desktop publishing systems have *already* changed my work as a fundraiser — profoundly. Like thousands of other fundraisers, I spend much of my time involved with written fundraising appeals, "letters" if you will. If I had available only the old Selectric typewriter I used to bang out magazine articles and science fiction stories twenty years ago — instead of the advanced computer system now on my desk at home — I'm dead certain I would write far less, and far less well. I would raise considerably less money, or even none at all. Can I prove that? No — but I *know* it's true. Computer technology has multiplied my productivity in the broadest and most meaningful sense of that term. Is it unreasonable, then, to expect that millenial advances in communications technologies will affect my work, and yours, any less?

That, I confess, is what's called a "rhetorical question"!

However, it's all well and good to talk about "emerging technologies," "broadband communications" and all the rest, and to predict they'll turn our lives upside down — but what does that *mean for me?* When I set out to write a fundraising appeal twenty years from now, what will I actually *do?* How will I use the "six keys to 21st Century fundraising" listed in the preceding chapter, creating appeals that are individualized, multi-sensory, information-rich, real-time, interactive and communal?

To explore these questions, I created the scenario that follows. Call it science fiction, if you will. This is my attempt to depict

TECHNOLOGY AND THE FUTURE OF FUNDRAISING

one typical daily experience in the life of a 21st Century fundraiser: what it might be like to write a fundraising letter in 2014. The seventeen "Cardinal Rules of Copywriting" below are similar to those I've written about elsewhere in giving advice to contemporary fundraisers — but they're oh, so very different!

1. Work at your desk and watch the wallscreen. Don't try to edit at a distance with your wrist- or pocket-comm. You can't see enough detail on those little screens. And the sound quality is simply awful!

2. Plug in your comm unit. Radio transmission isn't always reliable. And don't forget that solar batteries won't last forever. (Not even the sun will last *that* long!)

3. Press the "HELP!" button once to make sure it's working. You're never going to remember all this stuff without a little help!

4. Don't *write* the story: video's usually better. Precious few of your donors will actually read your letter. You've got to keep their attention. Use text and voice-over only when absolutely essential. If you don't have the footage, the Library of Congress will. Instruct your unit to search the public clip files.

5. Keep it short and simple. Half an hour is the most that *anyone* — even your most committed donor — will spend with your letter, no matter how brilliantly entertaining and informative. Most prospects will spend twenty seconds or less.

Fifty percent of your donors have requested a 1-2 minute executive summary only. (Just like a spot on the news shows, get it?)

Another 25% have set up their receivers to download hard-copy transcripts. (I think that's what they used to call "fax" transmissions — but grandma would have loved the color and special effects!)

Only 25% want a multimedia experience — and most of them will view only the items containing a few, carefully chosen key words.

But don't forget: you're really writing to reach that most important five percent who want to read it *all*. They include most of your very best donors. Chances are, they contribute more than half of your revenue. These are the people who will check out the newsclip file or the full report from your program staff — so be sure you don't forget to append them. Remember, too: by and large, these committed donors are the people who've joined your "insider's clubs"; they correspond with your program staff and with each other, and many of them participate in your ongoing focus groups — so they may even know more than you do about your organization's work!

6. Track your costs! Video rental and royalty charges mount up fast. Even those public-access Library of Congress royalties can add up.

7. Observe levels of confidentiality and donor commitment. Not everyone is entitled to know your organization's innermost secrets. And not everyone's interested! Besides, you don't want absolutely everyone to have access to your private toll-free lines; that's only for your very best donors. Tell your comm unit to "Key on donor commitment codes."

8. Remember: you're writing to 200,000 *individuals*. Don't ever use "you" in the plural (not even "you-all!" Regionalisms can be confusing in our polyglot society.) Write "Insert salutation here." And be sure to download all but the organization's most sensitive

··

program files into your privileged donors' accounts. Some may never forgive you if you don't.

9. Make your donors feel special. Be certain to run the personalization routines at least twice for your best donors, so you'll take advantage of every opportunity to customize the appeal to their unique concerns. Scan your file for overlooked or under-used types of personal information that may lend themselves to offhand references in your appeal, such as responses to a donor preference survey or demographic data that came to light when you merged your donor file with a public database.

10. Strictly limit the space you give to sponsors. Make sure the ads you run are appropriate for the audience: a spot for pizza or deodorant can look really strange in the middle of a High-Dollar pitch!

11. Don't use slang. Your translation program may have trouble finding the right equivalent in Eastern Spanish or Cantonese.

12. Remember to ask for money *tonight*. It may no longer be green, but it spends! If a donor doesn't authorize the transfer of funds tonight, she probably never will. Don't offer more than two payment options, or you may confuse her. Credit and debit accounts are usually more than enough.

13. Don't forget to sign your letter. This is a personal *letter*, not a newsletter or an annual report. If you don't have pre-recorded voice-text, customize a signature. It's rude to identify yourself only with the organization's logo. Try thinking of this as a letter to Mom and Dad from summer camp, and you *really* need the money!

14. When in doubt, look it up. Check all your facts in the Library. (Set it on automatic — if you trust the damn thing.) If there's even a shadow of doubt about anything, ask the Fundraising Expert.

....

Your organization's probably paying an arm and a leg to rent that program!

15. Before sending your letter, check everything twice. View all video clips. Listen to every soundbite. Review all voice-overs and transitions. Check your spelling, syntax, voice and video quality; the unit will do most of this for you automatically — but you've got to remember to *turn it on* when you begin to write your letter! And be certain to look for personalization errors. (You don't want to thank a deadbeat for a pledge she didn't fulfill!) Be absolutely certain your letter observes privacy protocols: you can be sued if you don't. And you're *personally* responsible!

16. Be careful with your merge-purge! Make sure your database is up-to-date. Sometimes, it can take 24 hours or more for your comm unit to download last night's address corrections and contribution data. And don't forget that some of your donors aren't on the fiber-optic net. You'll have to forward your letter and the list to a service bureau, so they can send out disks by surface mail in the morning.

17. Remember to register your letter with the Charities Agency. If it's not on file before you mail it, this may be the last fundraising letter you ever write!

TECHNOLOGY AND THE FUTURE OF FUNDRAISING

Visual Interlude D

On-Line Production Offers High-Tech Options Today

For many high-volume fundraising mailers, the future has been here for a number of years in the form of "on-line" production methods.

Every element of the four-color direct mail fundraising package pictured in part starting on page 53 was produced in one continuous, computer-mediated process on a single printing press. That's right: every element — letter, survey, insert, envelopes and all! Rolls of blank paper went in one end of the press; fully finished, correctly addressed fundraising letters came out the other end — bundled and sorted in proper order to achieve maximum postal discounts.

This marvel was accomplished on a specially equipped "web" printing press. (In printers' parlance, a "web" is a long roll of paper that streams at high speed between a press' rollers.) In this on-line process, the press was outfitted with components to glue, cut and fold as well as print the paper — plus "ink-jet" printers to personalize each package and a postage meter to affix the postal imprint. (The ink-jet produced those ragged, dot-matrix impressions. On the original, some appear in black ink, others in red.)

You may notice the envelopes appear to be printed on two different colors of paper. They actually are. Dan Suzio, my

production guru, tells me that, unlike most in-line systems, which use a single web, the press that produced this package ran two webs through simultaneously in parallel. One, consisting of tan paper stock, yielded up the Business Reply Envelope you see. The other web — beginning with plain white paper — was transformed into the other elements of the package, including the outer envelope. In the original, the carrier looks a lot like a Kraft envelope. The press created this impression by printing a golden color over most of the surface that was converted into the outer envelope, leaving blank white the rectangle on which the metered postage was affixed as well as the mailing-label-like element in the center; bright yellow and blue embellishments were added to dress up the "label."

Will wonders never cease? They're just beginning!

Now, a new wrinkle in printing technology holds promise of bringing the advantages of on-line printing — to the desktop. A new generation of printing presses uses digital technology to permit personalized, full-color printing in small press runs at a competitive cost. Using this new technology, it's possible to print 1,000 copies — or just 100 — of a brochure, a booklet or a case statement ... and personalize every one of them, varying the text and sometimes the graphics as well! The key to this new technology: unlike conventional web and sheet-fed presses, the new presses don't require printing plates; instead, text and graphic images are transferred digitally to the printing rollers that lay down ink on paper passing through.

· ·

*Some of these machines are priced as low as $200,000 — a
fraction of the cost of an on-line web press like the one that
produced the sample reproduced here, and well within the
budget of many large organizations that live by the printed
word. You say you're not running such a large organization?
Wait a few years: the new plateless presses may soon be
within your budget, too. And long before then, no doubt,
printers and specialized service bureaus will make the new
technology available at competitive rates.*

Coalition to Stop Gun Violence
100 Maryland Avenue, NE
Washington, D.C. 20002

National Opinion Survey On Gun Violence

Contents Prepared for:

Car-rt Sort   **CR 09

Mr. Mal Warwick
2723 Ashby Pl.
Berkeley, CA 94705-2353

COALITION TO STOP GUN VIOLENCE

100 Maryland Avenue, NE, Washington, DC 20002

(202) 544-7190

Coretta Scott King	Michael K. Beard
Honorary Chairperson	*Executive Director*

Dear Mr. Warwick,

Four years ago, Patrick Purdy walked up to an elementary school playground in California, and opened fire with his new AK47 assault rifle.

Today, I still wake up in a cold sweat.

As the teacher on duty at the playground, I can't forget how this deranged man systematically sprayed the black top six times with his semi-automatic assault weapon. And I vividly remember that the school doors were locked, so my children and I were corralled in like animals for the slaughter.

We had nowhere to run -- nowhere to hide. In less than two minutes, he was able to fire off 106 bullets at his helpless victims -- killing five children and wounding 29 others and myself.

Today, when I recall the screams of these children, I know that the greatest tragedy is not just what happened in my schoolyard that day.

The greatest tragedy is that America has done nothing to stop gun violence that kills, maims and terrorizes innocent citizens every day.

And there is only one reason why this violence is allowed to continue:

the NRA.

> The National Rifle Association is the most powerful special interest group in America. And the extremists who control the NRA spend more than $80 million a year to defeat each and every gun control proposal -- no matter how reasonable and important it is.
>
> The NRA's army of lobbyists even fought our efforts to ban machine guns, plastic pistols and cop-killer bullets that are specifically designed to pierce through bullet-proof vests!
>
> And the NRA defeated our proposal for a one week waiting period for gun sales. So law enforcement officers still don't have the time they need to see if a gun buyer has a criminal record or mental disorder -- before they walk away with the gun of their choice.

How do they get away with it? First, the NRA is bankrolled in large part by gun manufacturers and importers. Keep in mind, their 30 full-time lobbyists are also notorious for their arm-twisting tactics.

over, please ⟶

THE TIDE IS TURNING!

Americans are fed up. In the last few months, the Coalition to Stop Gun Violence has joined with outraged citizens to hand the NRA three major defeats that mean new hope for gun control in America.

Connecticut: Against an expensive and frenzied NRA lobbying campaign, the Coalition helped enact an outright ban on the sale and ownership of assault weapons in Connecticut.

New Jersey: When the NRA threatened to spend millions to defeat any legislator who opposed its position, the Coalition helped mobilize a massive public outcry. The result -- a near unanimous state Senate vote to continue the assault weapons ban.

Virginia: In a landmark battle to restrict gun traffic, the Coalition to Stop Gun Violence helped defeat the NRA and enact a one gun a month limit on handgun purchases in that state.

Over the last year, the Coalition to Stop Gun Violence has increased its membership tenfold. But our most important work is just beginning and we cannot succeed without the support of concerned citizens like you.

We can break the NRA control of gun laws in America -- but only if you are willing to take a stand. Please join in support the Coalition to Stop Gun Violence today.

Coalition to Stop Gun Violence
100 Maryland Avenue, NE
Washington, DC 20002
(202) 544-7190

National Opinion Survey on Gun Control Issues

Conducted by

COALITION TO STOP GUN VIOLENCE

for

BERKELEY, CALIFORNIA AND THE NATION

COALITION TO STOP GUN VIOLENCE
P.O. Box 9601
Washington, DC 20077-7193

Survey Participant:

Mr. Mal Warwick
~~2723 Ashby Pl~~
Berkeley, CA ~~94705-2352~~

Registered Survey #
CA1048267-LFPN315A

Response Deadline:

DECEMBER 3, 1993

Please take 30 seconds to answer these seven quick questions:

1. Do you favor a national law requiring a one week waiting period between the time a person applies to buy a gun and the time it's sold?

☐ YES   ☐ NO

2. Are you in favor of banning civilian use of assault weapons — that is, military-style guns that can hold up to 100 bullets?

☐ YES   ☐ NO

3. Do you favor stricter enforcement of current gun laws?

☐ YES   ☐ NO

4. Would you favor a national ban on cheap concealable handguns (Saturday Night Specials)?

☐ YES   ☐ NO

5. Which statement is closest to your opinion of the NRA (National Rifle Association)?
☐ Generally Positive
☐ Generally Negative
☐ The NRA is the main reason why America now lacks stronger gun control measures.

6. What is your current opinion of Congress on gun control issues?

☐ Very Positive
☐ Generally Positive
☐ Generally Negative
☐ Very Negative

7. Which statement below comes closest to your opinion about the 25,000 Americans who die each year by gun violence?
☐ It's sad, but it's the price we must pay for unrestricted guns.
☐ There's not much we can do about these deaths.
☐ We just need to make a greater effort to keep guns out of the hands of criminals and the insane. *
☐ We need to ban all assault weapons and handguns with limited exceptions allowed for the police, military, target shooters and collectors. *

* If you chose one of the last two statements to answer the last question, we need more than your survey results if we are going to win sensible gun control measures.

To take on the NRA and win, the Coalition to Stop Gun Violence needs the financial support of concerned Americans like you. So please take a moment now to write a check for $25, $50, $100 or more.
0133938449

► DETACH HERE ►

DETACH HERE ▶

▶

5. Which statement is closest to your opinion of the NRA (National Rifle Association)?
☐ Generally Positive
☐ Generally Negative
☐ The NRA is the main reason why America now lacks stronger gun control measures.

6. What is your current opinion of Congress on gun control issues?

*If you chose one of the last two statements to answer the last question, we need more than your survey results if we are going to win sensible gun control measures.

To take on the NRA and win, the Coalition to Stop Gun Violence needs the financial support of concerned Americans like you. So please take a moment now to write a check for $25, $50, $100 or more.

013349384449

✓ **YES, I'm for Gun Control...**
and I Want the Politicians to Stand Up to the NRA
and Pass Sensible Gun Control Laws!

That's why I have completed my survey, signed my petition to Congress, and enclosed a special contribution to the Coalition to Stop Gun Violence (or "CSGV") in the amount of:

☐ $25   ☐ $35   ☐ $50*   ☐ $100   ☐ $1000   ☐ Other $_____

* MR. WARWICK, YOUR $50 WILL HELP US BREAK THE NRA'S INFLUENCE ON CONGRESS.

Please make your check payable to CSGV and return it in the postage-paid envelope. To enable CSGV to lobby aggressively on your behalf for tough gun laws, your contribution is not tax-deductible.

PLEASE DO NOT DETACH.

Please send your petition, survey and check to CSGV. We will detach and personally deliver to Congress.

National Petition to the United States Congress

Dear Representative Ronald V. Dellums,

Whereas gun violence is a national problem, stopping gun violence should be a priority for the United States Congress.

Whereas assault weapons and Saturday Night Specials are the types of guns used most often in violent crimes, Congress should pass legislation banning these guns.

Whereas there is no reason why we should let criminals buy 5, 10 or 50 guns a month, we need a national law restricting gun purchases to one a month (unless authorized by law enforcement officials.)

I respectfully urge the Members of Congress to work for this crucial legislation to stem the tide of violent bloodshed in this country.

Sincerely,

LFPN315A   Mr. Mal Warwick

MR. MRL WARWICK

LFPN315R

BERKELEY, CA 94705-2513

PLEASE EXPEDITE:
Congressional Petition
Enclosed

You can help CSGV even more by using your own First Class stamps on this envelope. Thank you. →

Your contribution will help offset the NRA's $80 million advantage!

BUSINESS REPLY MAIL

FIRST CLASS MAIL   PERMIT NO. 19114   WASHINGTON, DC

POSTAGE WILL BE PAID BY ADDRESSEE

NO POSTAGE
NECESSARY
IF MAILED
IN THE
UNITED STATES

Coalition to Stop Gun Violence
P.O. Box 96011
Washington, DC 20077-7193

MR. WARWICK,

*Don't be silent while the gun fanatics
dictate the policies of our government.
Join with the Coalition to Stop Gun Violence
by supporting our campaign for a comprehensive
handgun ban in America today.*

PLEASE RESPOND BY: DECEMBER 3, 1993

PEERING INTO THE FUTURE OF DIRECT RESPONSE FUNDRAISING

4

TECHNOLOGY AND THE FUTURE OF FUNDRAISING

::

I n the preceding chapters, I've attempted to look well past the horizon, squinting down through twenty years of unforesee-able events to discern the nature of the work that you and I may be doing far in the future. To know for sure whether my predictions are valid, you'll have to wait — for as long as two decades!

Is this exercise *useful?* I don't know. For me, the effort to peer into the future is worthwhile in its own right: for its intellectual content, for its value in helping to shape our organizations' strategic plans — and for sheer fun.

However, to make use of the information in this little book — to convert it into *knowledge* — it's important to step back from the future and examine what's here and now a little more closely. Clearly, forces well beyond our control are reshaping the environment we'll be working in for many years to come — starting *now*. For you and me to anticipate the effects of those forces — to consider changing how we do our work — we need look more carefully at *today's* trends. That's what I propose to do in this concluding essay.

Here, then, are a few of the major implications I see for practitioners of direct mail fundraising — both consultants and in-house staff members at nonprofits — as today's emerging tech-nologies come into wider use:

›   Like other organizations, both government agencies and private businesses, nonprofits are likely to find "out-sourcing" attractive and cost-effective in the years ahead. Learning about and managing these new technologies is technically demanding and will require specialized skills not widely available for many years, if ever. So, despite a current trend among charities to bring their direct mail fundraising programs in-house, they will continue to seek the services of outside vendors — not just for consultation and new ideas but, in many areas, for hands-on services as well.

› Today, direct mail fundraising services are provided largely by specialized consulting firms, in-house agencies at nonprofits and solo consultants. A few printing companies, lettershops and database management firms and a handful of major direct response advertising agencies offer some competition. In the years ahead, however, as complex and expensive new technologies come into wider use in the field, the range of service providers will broaden — and the lines of demarcation among them will blur.

› The complexity and the capital costs of new technologies will make it impossible for all but a handful of very large organizations to maintain in-house the full range of necessary services to keep their programs humming. This will lead to the rapid growth of business alliances, both formal and informal, sometimes including nonprofits as well as consulting firms and other vendors. These alliances may involve joint marketing or merchandising arrangements or shared capital; among for-profit ventures, they might entail overlapping leadership in a fashion now widely associated with Japanese business.

› The advent of new technologies has profound personal implications for all those employed in direct mail fundraising — and not just for employers. We'll all need to master planning, decision-making and production techniques that few now understand. Intensive on-the-job training — and perhaps formal, mid-career education as well — will be essential for any manager who wishes to stay on top of the field.

TECHNOLOGY AND THE FUTURE OF FUNDRAISING

› Despite substantial growth in telefundraising and in the use of video, direct response TV and Electronic Funds Transfer, most transactions in direct mail fundraising today are conducted by mail. The U.S. Postal Service delivers the lion's share of all fund appeals and is the means for nearly all donors to return gifts to the charities and causes of their choice. But this will change — gradually in the 1990s, and more quickly after the turn of the century. Soon, it will no longer be adequate for a direct response fundraising agency to understand direct mail alone.

› Demographic trends and other influences at work in U.S. society will help intensify the competition for voluntary contributions and thus accelerate the use of New Wave technologies to conduct genuine "relationship marketing." Today most donors — and virtually *all* direct mail donors — are treated as members of a "segment" or class, based on a vague characterization of their behavior as donors. Relationship marketing requires that they be treated as individuals with unique values, preferences and histories. The sophisticated data management and production techniques now on the horizon will make this possible, helping fundraisers generate even larger sums from an already generous public.

But how? What can you and I do — *today* — to help realize the promise of this hopeful view of the future? I have six suggestions:

1. Calculate the **Long-Term Value** of your donors — and invest in increasing that value. Consider such devices as new-donor welcome packages, segmented newsletters and dedicated in-house donor service telephone lines. Offer a monthly giving and at least one High-Dollar giving club, if you don't already.

2. Take a fresh look at your donor file **segmentation**. If you're not segmenting at all now, use Recency, Frequency and Giving Level to do so. If you segment using these basic criteria, then test other variables, too, such as the number of years donors have been on file or the medium through which you acquired them. Or try measuring the difference between those who only respond to membership renewal notices versus those who respond only to special appeals.

3. Use **market research** tools such as surveys and focus groups to learn more about your donors — and act on the information! Both quantitative research (including surveys and polls) and qualitative (especially focus groups) have their uses. If you haven't participated in donor research programs like this, you may be astonished by what you learn when you do.

4. Explore **Electronic Funds Transfer**. There are ways even the smallest nonprofit organization can build a monthly sustainer program using this state-of-the-art fundraising technique. Check out one of the several companies nationwide that now offer such services.

5. Review your **donor involvement** programs — and beef them up. Consider an insider's newsletter, special briefings, receptions or travel opportunities for top donors — or call them to ask their opinions about the issue or program to feature in your next appeal.

6. Make certain your organization conducts itself and all its fundraising activities with the strictest regard for **ethics**. In the long run, donors simply won't settle for anything less — and we shouldn't, either.

Follow this advice, or ignore it — as you will. Nothing will *really* prepare you for the changes to come, in any event.

TECHNOLOGY AND THE FUTURE OF FUNDRAISING

. . . .

But whatever your opinion, whatever your feelings, whatever you do or don't, you can count on one thing for sure about the future: Things are going to be different.

TECHNOLOGY AND THE FUTURE OF FUNDRAISING

High-Dollar Packaging Accentuates "High-Touch"

Please don't walk away with the impression that I advocate using fancy technology for its own sake. To my mind, high-tech methods are worthy of fundraisers' attention only if they help us do our jobs more cost-effectively — and thus ultimately raise more money — or if they help strengthen the bonds between us and our donors.

In some circumstances, the high-tech, on-line production methods described in the preceding visual interlude (see pp. 50-58) help fundraisers build relationships with donors — because they allow us to insert more personal information in our appeals than we might otherwise be able to use. In acquisition packages like the one reproduced starting on page 70, the principal value of that personal information is that using it opens up myriad possibilities for donors to become involved — by doing something like completing and returning a survey as well as sending a check. And personalized "involvement devices" frequently boost response rates, sometimes very substantially, so we know they work!

But there's another side to the question of donor involvement. Contemporary on-line packages — like other formats familiar to millions of Americans as "junk mail" —

send a clear message to donors: they're not being treated as individuals. It's no coincidence that today on-line packages are most frequently used in grassroots lobbying efforts; if you want to influence the United States Congress, you'll expect to be treated as one of many, not as an individual.

If you want your donors to feel you're approaching them as the thinking, caring individuals they are, you'll need to use different technology — to create a high-touch effect that can be equally involving. That effect is illustrated by the High-Dollar fundraising package reproduced beginning on the page facing this one.

In this two-dimensional, black-and-white reproduction, it's hard to tell how the appeal fosters involvement, so I'll do my best to describe some of what's going on:

The outer envelope, which measures 9 x 12", is a warm, bright purple color. The paper stock is thick and heavily textured — resulting in tactile involvement the moment the reader fishes it out of the mail.

The mailing label, printed in red ink, is one of the "peel-off" variety. It's addressed using what appears to be a typewriter. That's involving because it really gives the impression that a live human being sat down somewhere to type the label, thus setting up the preconditions for a genuine dialogue between the reader and the signer of the letter inside.

The postage stamps are real, and one of them is a colorful commemorative. This reinforces the impression that the

....

contents have some personal character and bear no resemblance to junk mail.

Paper-clipped to the first page of the letter is a four-color portrait of a Guatemalan woman in brilliantly-hued traditional garb. That paper clip is involving, too, because the reader has to take it off in order to read the letter — and because a real person had to put it on in the first place.

This is, of course, a personalized letter. At least, it's personally addressed and bears a specific date. The copy's involving, too: warm, direct and informative. And everything's typed, fortifying the personal character of the appeal.

The reply device is also personalized. It's printed on thick, lightly-textured recycled stock.

That's a "live" postage stamp on the reply envelope, which also appears to be typed.

This package, developed by my colleague, Julie Levak, at Mal Warwick & Associates, is an outstanding example of how "high-touch" elements can be put to work in a high-tech world. Naturally, producing and mailing this package was highly labor-intensive, and very expensive: someone had to collate all those personalized elements by hand — and someone had to put on all those paper clips!

But here's the secret to this package: it wouldn't have been possible without advanced technology.

TECHNOLOGY AND THE FUTURE OF FUNDRAISING

Sound crazy? Think about this: how did MADRE know
which people to send this package to? They'd have been
nuts to spend all that money on painstaking hand labor if
they were going to mail it out at random to people listed in
the phone book. The secret, then, was in the selection of an
appropriate list of likely prospects — which was only
possible because of all the computer work that preceded this
mailing! So, in this case at least, high-tech yielded
high-touch.

TECHNOLOGY AND THE FUTURE OF FUNDRAISING

MADRE
FOR THE CHILDREN

WOMEN'S PEACE NETWORK
121 WEST 27th STREET
ROOM 301
NEW YORK, NEW YORK 10001

Mr. John Doe
123 Any Street
Any Town, AS 00000

MADRE
FOR THE CHILDREN

121 WEST 27th STREET
ROOM 301
NEW YORK, NEW YORK 10001

VIVIAN STROMBERG, EXECUTIVE DIRECTOR

Mr. John Doe
123 Any Street
Any Town, AS 00000

Dear Mr. Doe,

I'm writing you and a few
have demonstrated deep compass
America.

Because I need you to jo
role in an ambitious campaign
the small Guatemalan village

Xemal is in the Western
home to many of the indigeno
poverty and repression are e

With your help today
sponsoring this proj
a weaving cooperativ
women and their chil

... and the knowledge that they will be able to
turn their lives -- and indeed the life of their
village -- around.

MADRE is working with the women of Xemal who want to
become economically self-sufficient with work they can do in
their own village. This is such a hopeful project because it
will provide a better life for so many women and children in
Guatemala.

Let me give you just a few reasons why we at MADRE have
chosen to devote so much of our energy to helping the women and
children of Guatemala:

>> Over the past ten years, tens of thousands
of indigenous people have been killed through
torture, "disappearances" and the scorched earth
campaigns that characterize the Guatemalan military.

>> Due to the repression, more than 46,000 women

RECYCLED PAPER

MADRE
FOR THE CHILDREN

121 WEST 27th STREET
ROOM 301
NEW YORK, NEW YORK 10001

VIVIAN STROMBERG, EXECUTIVE DIRECTOR

April 22, 1992

Mr. John Doe
123 Any Street
Any Town, AS 00000

Dear Mr. Doe,

   I'm writing you and a few very committed individuals who
have demonstrated deep compassion for the people of Central
America.

   Because I need you to join me in playing a _special founding
role_ in an ambitious campaign to help women and their children in
the small Guatemalan village of Xemal.

   Xemal is in the Western Plateau region of Guatemala. It is
home to many of the indigenous _Mam_ people. It is a region where
poverty and repression are extreme.

        With your help today MADRE, the organization
        sponsoring this project, will be able to establish
        a _weaving cooperative_ that will enable hundreds of
        women and their children to face the future with hope ...

        ... and _the knowledge that they will be able to
        turn their lives_ -- and indeed the life of their
        village -- _around._

   MADRE is working with the women of Xemal who want to
become economically self-sufficient with work they can do in
their own village. This is such a hopeful project because it
will provide a better life for so many women and children in
Guatemala.

   Let me give you just a few reasons why we at MADRE have
chosen to devote so much of our energy to helping the women and
children of Guatemala:

        >> Over the past ten years, tens of thousands
        of indigenous people have been killed through
        torture, "disappearances" and the scorched earth
        campaigns that characterize the Guatemalan military.

        >> Due to the repression, more than 46,000 women

RECYCLED PAPER

are widows and more than 120,000 children are
orphans.

>> And it is the women who bear the responsibility
for providing the food, clothing, education,
shelter and nurturing for their children.

This weaving project will help the very determined women
of Xemal to develop the skills to provide a better life for
themselves and their children --

-- and then pass those skills on to the next generation.

To help the women of the village of Xemal will require an
ongoing commitment from MADRE. And with your help now we can
meet that commitment.

I know that, working together, we will succeed because I've
been a part of this unique organization for eight years. In that
time we have accomplished remarkable things -- by acting in the
true spirit of love and friendship for women and children in many
parts of world.

MADRE was founded in 1983 to respond to the urgent needs of
Nicaraguan children who were suffering and dying because of the
U.S.-supported Contra War.

Our first delegation to Nicaragua delivered baby cereal and
powdered milk to women and their children.

Over the years MADRE formed strong bonds of friendship
with the women and children of Nicaragua, enabling us to support
Nicaragua's first women's hospital as well as several health care
projects in the countryside.

We've also supported life-saving projects in El Salvador to
help children there who've suffered from decades of poverty and
repression.

And just a few months ago I led a special delegation of
MADRE women to Iraq where we delivered ten tons of milk and
medicine for Iraqi children who continue to die from disease
and malnutrition -- the aftereffects of the U.S.-led bombing
and ongoing sanctions against their country.

For the past eight years, MADRE has worked with women
from different nations to build a world community for all our
children. We work to replace the pain and suffering caused by
our government's policies with friendship and hope.

So many caring people have come forward over the years.

MADRE's supporters include actors Joanne Woodward and Alfre
Woodard, Susan Sarandon and Raul Julia, as well as prize-winning

authors Alice Walker, Kurt Vonnegut and Toni Morrison -- among so many others.

With friends like these, MADRE has been able to send over $2 million in supplies and services directly to those most hurt by poverty, war and repression.

I ask you today to join me in this campaign of friendship and hope -- by giving the children of Xemal, Guatemala, a chance for tomorrow.

You can do that by becoming a member of the Xemal Weaving Cooperative's "Founders Circle."

Let me tell you more about what this project can accomplish -- with your founding support:

MADRE will help provide the <u>looms</u>, <u>materials</u> and <u>stipends</u> for the instructors to train thirty women to work on industrial-size looms.

They will weave woolen fabric in traditional patterns and then embroider them with the traditional motifs of the Mam culture.

By learning to weave their beautiful, colorful traditional patterns on industrial looms, they will be able to create enough volume to sell their fabric and clothing on the domestic market and, with MADRE's help, in the United States.

The village will provide the structures to house two weaving centers. MADRE will provide the looms and class furniture, wool, thread, transportation costs for the women, and stipends for two teachers.

The first thirty women to be trained, all heads of households, will be able to support a total of 285 dependents -- children and the elderly.

Once the Weaving Cooperative is up and running, MADRE will help them market their beautiful weavings in the U.S.

In time, the Xemal Weaving Cooperative could provide the economic foundation for the village -- supporting the building of a local school, fostering the creation of a local market, and helping the people of that village maintain their traditions and their way of life.

I hope that you will be a part of this very special MADRE effort -- by joining the Xemal Weaving Cooperative's "Founders Circle."

Your Founder's Gift today will help pay for the looms, wool

and thread, and tables and chairs for the first stage of the project.

Total cost for this stage of the Xemal project is $62,000.

We do need to raise this amount over the next seven weeks so we can meet the commitment we made to the women and children.

So I hope you will make your special Founding Gift today.

When you become a Founder of the Xemal Weaving Cooperative, with a Founding Gift of $1,000 or more, I'll see that you get a beautiful example of the traditional weavings that you will help make possible.

Your Founding Gift for the Weaving Cooperative is truly a gift of friendship and hope, and I thank you in advance for your love and concern.

For the children,

Vivian Stromberg
Executive Director

P.S. Please join us today with your Founding Gift for the Xemal Weaving Cooperative so we will be able to deliver our gift in the next few months. If you can be so generous as to provide a special Founding Gift of $1,000 we'll send you a beautiful traditional weaving from Guatemala.

```
To:    Vivian Stromberg,
       Executive Director
       MADRE

From:  Mr. John Doe
       123 Any Street
       Any Town, AS 00000


                                        34DOE


RE:    GUATEMALA WEAVING PROJECT
       Founders Circle


Dear Vivian,  Yes, I want to join you as a Founder
of the Weaving Cooperative in Xemal, Guatemala --
to help hundreds of women and children who suffer
from war and poverty.

I understand my special Founding Gift will enable
the women of Guatemala to begin a weaving industry
that will help them provide for their children --
and bring about the economic renewal of their village.

I'm rushing my Founding Gift today so you will be
able to help provide looms, wool, thread, and class
materials to the women of Xemal in the next few
months.

[  ]  $1,000   Enclosed is my Founding Gift.  Please
      send me a beautiful example of the traditional
      weavings of Guatemala.

[  ]  I cannot join the Founders Circle at this time
      but would like to make a contribution of:
      $_____.
```

MADRE
FOR THE CHILDREN 121 WEST 27th STREET
ROOM 301
NEW YORK, NEW YORK 10001

MADRE
FOR THE CHILDREN

121 WEST 27th STREET
ROOM 301
NEW YORK, NEW YORK 10001

29 USA

Vivian Stromberg
MADRE
Women's Peace Network
121 West 27th St., Room 301
New York, New York 10001

RECYCLED PAPER

AN ANNOTATED READING LIST

5

I f you read a lot about new technology and its impact on the world around us, you'll find many familiar names and titles in the pages that follow.

If you're unfamiliar with recent writing in this field, you'll consider many of my sources obscure, or at least difficult to find. There are dozens of books in this list, most of them readily available in libraries, but finding some of the periodicals (and a few of the books) may be challenging. Nonetheless, I've included the usual bibliographic notations to help you on your way, just in case you want to track them down.

Whatever your previous reading in this field, however, I *don't* intend the following bibliography to be used primarily as a list of suggested reading. Rather, this is my effort to distill what was most interesting and significant to me from my varied reading about emerging technologies over the last couple of years; with few exceptions, the entries are annotated with my brief summary or, in some cases, comments. I viewed the subject through the lens of my professional perspective — as a fundraiser specializing in direct response, and as a businessperson and consultant to nonprofit organizations. If you're who I think you are, you share at least some aspects of that perspective.

In other words, you don't *have* to read the books and articles listed here. For the most part, my comments and summaries may be adequate. I hope so.

There are 178 books, articles and newspaper stories catalogued in the pages that follow. I've grouped the material into nine

categories, arranged in descending order of usefulness to someone
who shares my interest in fundraising and nonprofits:

› The future of nonprofit organizations

› High-tech marketing

› Technology in the business world

› Social impact of emerging technologies

› Networking

› The coming convergence

› Video and multimedia

› Trends and trend-meisters

› Bells, whistles and breakthroughs

Most of these categories are self-explanatory, and I rarely
had to make arbitrary choices in apportioning individual entries
among them. But the lines increasingly blur as the list goes on. The
ninth category ("Bells, whistles and breakthroughs") is focused on
specific products but contains entries about other items that didn't
fit well in any other category.

No entry appears in more than one category.

Enjoy!

The future of nonprofit organizations

Barringer, Felicity. "In the Worst of Times, America Keeps Giving," *New York Times* (March 15, 1992), p. E6. With charitable giving continuing on a steady course upward, claiming an ever-greater share of Americans' disposable income, the long-term outlook for nonprofit institutions and organizations is extremely encouraging. "In the next 10 to 15 years," says Waldemar A. Nielsen, who studied charitable foundations, "we could see a massive increase of resources in the nonprofit world.

Chen, Ingfei. "New Main Library to Take Big Technological Leap," *San Francisco Chronicle*. A "wonderland of technology that will someday bring the library into every home in the city." "The computer network would list the city's 18 million books, periodicals, photographs, clippings and other documents and eventually tap into other library resources in the Bay Area — and, someday, perhaps even around the world. A few clicks at a keyboard would also pull up government documents with information, for example, on how to apply for a dog license."

Craver, Roger. "Politics: Igniting a Political Revolution," *Fund Raising Management* (April 1989), pp. 88-92. "Direct mail provided a new and uniquely accessible medium of political communication, offering voters genuine recourse and a safety valve for steaming political emotions."

Green, Alan, editor. "Communicating Today: Serving Nonprofit Needs with Technology." Benton Foundation (1986). This unpublished paper presented eight brief scenarios describing how nonprofit organizations used telecommunications to further their work in the mid-80s: "live bilingual training programs broadcast via satellite," "a videoconference linking [an association's] constituents across the country with [its] biennial convention," "a live satellite link-up" between the U.S. and the U.S.S.R., "a temporary network of cable systems that offered viewers in the South in-depth coverage of the 1984 presidential primary campaign," plus several videoconferences, including one with call-in questions that was carried by 250 public and cable TV stations in 45 states.

· ·

Greene, Stephen G. "Technology: Are Charities Missing the Revolution?" *Chronicle of Philanthropy* (October 19, 1993), pp. 1, 26-30. "The 'information superhighway' could overhaul how non-profits operate, but few of them are ready for the changes to come... The new technology will allow non-profits to receive donations electronically, have their own cable-television channels, and use sophisticated computer and telecommunications systems to conduct much of their business — from holding board meetings to submitting grant proposals... But it is still far from clear whether non-profit groups — and the people they serve — will have cheap and easy access to the 'information superhighway'... Some experts are afraid non-profits could lose out because they are not doing much to influence debate over how the information highway will be configured and who will own it." This article is worth reading in entirety; it's written with the *Chronicle's* usual thoroughness and focus on the big picture. There are insights in this piece I wouldn't have expected from a journalistic overview. For example: "Some experts predict that direct mail will be useful primarily to supplement electronic messages." Quoting Roger Craver: "'[I]t will be far more cost-efficient to distribute information electronically,' particularly as postage and paper costs continue to rise."

——————. *Chronicle of Philanthropy* (October 19, 1993). "Few Foundations Make Grants to Help Non-Profits With Information Technology." The key exceptions, according to Greene, are the Benton Foundation, John D. and Catherine T. MacArthur Foundation, Pew Charitable Trusts and the John & Mary R. Markle Foundation. Greene also notes that "information about foundations has become available through computer networks." He cites the Environmental Grantmakers Association of 150 foundations, which list their grants through EcoNet, run by the Institute for Global Communications in San Francisco.

Hodgkinson, Virginia A., Richard A. Lyman, and Associates. *The Future of the Nonprofit Sector: Challenges, Changes, and Policy Considerations.* San Francisco: Jossey-Bass Publishers, 1989. Hardcover, 507 pages. I haven't read this one yet. It's just the sort of academic treatment I've shunned, whenever possible, through all the nearly 30 years since I liberated myself from graduate school.

TECHNOLOGY AND THE FUTURE OF FUNDRAISING

LaPlante, Alice. "Center for Missing Children Adopts Multimedia Tech," *Infoworld* (July 13, 1992), page 50. "A PC-based multimedia system [is used by the National Center for Missing & Exploited Children to] send high-resolution color photographs of missing children to law enforcement agencies around the country within minutes, if not seconds... The system was designed to deliver the highest resolution images possible to any Group 3 fax machine in the world." For *any* nonprofit involved in distributing time-sensitive visual information, the potential of this technology is staggering.

Magid, Lawrence J. "Computer File: 'Mentors' Aid Nonprofit Groups," *Los Angeles Times* (March 7, 1991). San Francisco-based CompuMentor and its affiliates in other cities match nonprofit organizations with volunteer 'mentors' to make more effective use of technology.

Miller, Rockley L. "Learning Benefits of Interactive Technologies," unpublished (distributed at the Library of Congress National Demonstration Laboratory), 1992, 2 pages. Miller is identified as Editor and Publisher of *The Videodisc Monitor* and President of the Interactive Video Industry Association. "A typical cost-per-student break-even point for interactive instruction might occur when from 100 to 200 students are using a program. Beyond that number, savings build dramatically. In one example, Federal Express expects to save over $100 million by using interactive systems for employee training."

Nicholson, Margie. *Cable Access: Community Channels and Productions for Nonprofits.* Washington, D.C.: Benton Foundation, 1990. Softcover, 59 pages. An introductory how-to manual for nonprofit organizations in general and community groups in particular in the use of cable TV technology. Part I is "Why Use Cable Access: Recognizing Access Opportunities," Part II is "How to Use Cable Access: Strategies for Matching Your Needs With Access Opportunities" and Part III consists of 12 "Case Studies." There's a resource list in the appendix.

Payne, Eloise T. "The Action Is Interactive," *Foundation News* (March-April 1991), pp. 58-60. "Move over, TVs and VCRs: interactive media are taking center stage. Foundations can help ensure that education and training are among the beneficiaries."

....

Sherman, Tom. *Electronic Networking for Nonprofit Groups: A Guide to Getting Started.* Cupertino, California and Washington, D.C.: Apple Community Affairs and the Benton Foundation, 1991. Softcover, 45 pages. A readable, how-to manual in the central, enabling technology of computer networking. Part I is entitled "Understanding Electronic Networking," Part II is "Choosing and Using Electronic Networks." There's also a useful Appendix that includes examples, a planning checklist and a list of support and training resources.

Shuman, Bruce A. *The Library of the Future: Alternative Scenarios for the Information Profession.* Englewood, Colorado: Libraries Unlimited, Inc., 1989. Hardcover, 140 pages. From one perspective, this book represents a strong argument that librarians should catalog books, not write them. However, despite deadly prose and a mechanistic structure, Shuman presents an interesting series of vignettes of the 21st-century world. He discusses nine scenarios — two utopian, four dystopian, and three "incrementalist" pictures of the role (or non-existence) of public libraries 15 to 30 years in the future.

Stehle, Vince. "Volunteer Computer Help for Non-Profits," *Chronicle of Philanthropy* (June 4, 1991), pp. 29-31. "San Francisco group has arranged over 1,000 matches between experts and charities; now it's helping to start such programs in other cities." All about CompuMentor, founded in 1986.

Stepp, Laura Sessions. "Focus on Self Has Changed Language of Sacrifice," *Washington Post* (March 24, 1991), pp. A20-21. "Charitable groups report attitude of giving to feel good, not giving until it hurts... Historian Arthur Schlesinger Jr. said Americans are at the end of a 30-year cycle of self-absorption. But he sees signs that generosity may be coming back in style."

Turner, Anne. "It Ain't Real But Send Money," *California Libraries* (March 1992), pp. 5, 18. About the "virtual library"— "a library without walls,"..."a library in which computerized information retrieval techniques link the user to much larger collections of information than are present in the computer at hand."

TECHNOLOGY AND THE FUTURE OF FUNDRAISING

Warwick, Mal. "Fund Raising on the Road to the 21st Century," *Fund Raising Management* (January 1992), pp. 28-29. Sixteen trends for direct mail fundraising in the 1990s — including the prediction that the future will be full of surprises.

—————. *Revolution in the Mailbox: How Direct Mail Fundraising Is Changing the Face of American Society — And How Your Organization Can Benefit.* Berkeley, California: Strathmoor Press, 1990. Hardcover, 313 pages. (Okay, so I couldn't resist the temptation to plug my own book.) In the book's final chapter, "Fundraising for the 21st Century," I attempted to grapple with some of the larger questions about the future of nonprofit fundraising and communications, exploring a vision of direct response fundraising in the "wired nation" of the next century.

Withrow, Kirti. "LC's Newest Addition to Its Vision for the Future: National Demonstration Laboratory to Open in March," *LC Information Bulletin* (February 24, 1992), pp. 73-76. "LC," it turns out, is the Library of Congress, and the full name of the laboratory referenced in the subtitle is "The National Demonstration Laboratory for Interactive Information Technology." The Library of Congress is devoting a lot of resources to readying itself for the future; I believe you and I will be the beneficiaries in years to come.

High-tech marketing

Craver, Roger. "Step Into the Future," *Target Marketing* (August 1990), pp. 12-14. "A golden age of direct marketing is about to dawn for those who begin preparing now" to come to grips with :the coming reality of instant communications" and other epochal forces reshaping American society.

Deloitte & Touche. *A Special Report on the Impact of Technology on Direct Marketing in the 1990s.* New York: Direct Marketing Association, 1990. Softcover, 104 pages. This well-organized study — intended to provide guideposts to direct marketers in considering investments in new technologies in the period 1990-94 — leads with three now-infamous quotations that make clear how very unpredictable the course of future technological developments can be. The most interesting is this one: "The probable simplification of the facsimile system ... must sooner or later interfere ... with the transportation of letters by the slower means of the post." The Postmaster General of the United States, 1872." "Perhaps the key finding of the study is that the direct marketing industry has not widely absorbed important technologies." Discusses technology under four headings: data and information management (database technologies, expert systems and neural networks, workstations); communications and interactive media (ISDN, 900-numbers, Interactive Voice Response); creative and production technology (desktop publishing, color electronic prepress systems, ink-jet customization, selective binding and inserting); customer transaction and fulfillment (barcoding and scanning, electronic data interchange, radio frequency technology).

Eckhouse, John. "The High-Tech Future of Advertising," *San Francisco Chronicle* (no date: dog ate it), pp. B1, B8. "Technological advances in the Information Age drastically may affect the advertising industry, forcing it to reach out to individuals instead of the mass market." "Many viewers of the future can be expected to spend an inordinate amount of time switching channels, and little or no time watching TV commercials. 'That kind of viewer empowerment scares advertising agencies,'" an ad man said. 'It creates more fragmented audiences, making it harder to reach a mass audience.'" What Eckhouse implies (but doesn't quite say) is that the principal implication of the whiz-bang new multimedia technologies and the fabled 800 TV channels is *not* its power to overwhelm the public with an ever-growing volume of information. Rather, what's most important is the power of technology to carry "personalization" to the ultimate expression: "one-on-one marketing."

Hall, Carl T. "Postal Service to Face More Competition: Electronic Alternatives Expect More Business," *San Francisco Chronicle* (March 6, 1992), pp. B1, B20. Electronic messaging via Fax, voice-mail and E-mail is growing fast. "And while the price of stamps keeps going up, the cost of electronic gadgets and telephone service has been coming down for years." "The full cost of the average business letter, labor included, is estimated to be about $10 to $12, compared with less than $5 for a computer version transmitted electronically."

TECHNOLOGY AND THE FUTURE OF FUNDRAISING

————————. "Junk Mail that Fits in a VCR: Marketers Put Ads on Video Cassettes," *San Francisco Chronicle*, pp. C1, C6. "Producing a professional-quality video and distributing it to a mass audience isn't cheap. It may cost more than $5 a copy just to reproduce a program-length tape. For a short commercial spot, the price drops to $2 or less, but production can run anywhere from $10,000 to more than $100,000, depending on how elaborate the project."

Hitchcock, Doglas R. "Plugging Into Interactive Sources: Should You Get Wired?", *Circulation Management* (September 1993), pp. 44-48. "Though direct mail's hardly in imminent danger of being replaced, a wide range of magazines are already marketing subscriptions and single copies through computer networks — and preparing to be part of the coming revolution in two-way media." One key insight: "For most publishers — especially smaller ones... — the key to successful network circulation marketing appears to be attracting users to the magazine first by offering gratis information. Often, this involves posting press releases on computer bulletin boards, uploading stories from current issues, and providing back issues for network databases. Giving away information also helps marketers comply with remaining restrictions that prohibit purely commercial ventures on some networks."

Holusha, John. "Technology: Gutenberg Goes Digital," *New York Times* (December 5, 1993), page F-11. "A new generation of [printing] presses is emerging that eliminates the metal plates, creating flexibility that should allow shorter press runs and even let the publisher make on-the-fly changes. A full-color advertising circular, for example, could carry a message tailored to each individual customer... The faster plateless color presses might crank out 100 to 10,000 copies of a booklet, brochure or annual report, industry experts say, while above 10,000 metal-plate techniques would probably still be more economical." Costs run $200,000 to $500,000 for machines from two manufacturers, one Israeli, the other Belgian. One consultant predicts "digital operations [will] spring up near airports, so that salesmen and marketing specialists will not have to drag heavy bags of brochures."

....

Huntsinger, Jerry. "Direct Mail: Sweeping Changes Since 1969," *Fund Raising Management* (April 1989), pp. 64-68. Check out the charts I've included in this book that depict changes in direct mail technologies over the past two decades; you'll get the drift of Jerry's argument from them.

Jaffee, Larry. "Mail-by-Computer Favored by 21% of Survey Respondents, Says IEEE," *DM News* (October 18, 1993), page 7. "Twenty-one percent of respondents to a national phone survey about technology said they'd be 'very interested' in receiving mail via computer, while 23 percent checked off 'somewhat interested... The younger the adult, the more receptive he or she would be to computer-delivered mail."

Lazar, William; Priscilla La Barbera; James M. MacLachlan; and Allen E. Smith. *Marketing 2000 and Beyond.* Chicago, Illinois: American Marketing Association, 1990. Hardcover, 246 pages. Here,. in another product of writing by committee, is a compendium of articles beginning "With the Future in Mind." The book is a product of an American Marketing Association research project on the future of marketing. Marshall McLuhan is quoted at the outset: "We're driving faster and faster into the future, trying to steer by using only the rear-view mirror." An important insight to keep in mind when trying to predict the shape and direction of things to come! The book's chapter on technological change is a brief survey of new technologies and contains little new insight. The authors' overall perspective is summed up thus (p. 6): "...economies of scale, particularly those associated with mass production, may be modified and overridden by considerations of increasing customization and individualization of products, enhancing consumer satisfaction and expanding consumer choices." Nonprofit managers take note: there's no such thing as a "mass market" anymore!

Morris-Lee, James. "New Technology Helps Marketers Get Personal," *Direct Marketing* (February 1992), pp. 20-23. "Direct mail is moving from mere personalization to cost-effective custom communication with a new technology that lets computers talk directly to printing presses — and has marketers talking once again about the kind of response rates they've always dreamed about."

TECHNOLOGY AND THE FUTURE OF FUNDRAISING

Ostrager, Gary. "High-Tech Marketing: Advanced Technology and Customer Service," *DM News* (April 6, 1992), pp. 29, 48. "Everyone pays lip service to customer service. But few firms take full advantage of the tools at their disposal to meet consumers' tangible and intangible needs. Gary Ostrager explores some of these high-tech options — like the advanced kiosks used by Florsheim and the smart carts he predicts will be used by auto manufacturers — and explains the importance of the management philosophy behind them." "In the not-too-distant future," Ostrager writes, "you'll flick on a switch on the car console and be linked to the dealer's computer service system for an online diagnostics test, performed overnight. The next morning, a light is blinking on the console. It's your electronic mailbox. The dealer's computer service system indicates a need for service."

Rapp, Stan. "Welcome to One-to-one Publishing," *DM News* (December 15, 1986), pp. 18, 54. "The May 1984 issue of *Farm Journal*, with a circulation of 900,000, had 8,896 different versions, each with its own special combination of advertising and editorial, and all printed on high-speed presses at a production cost not too far above conventional publishing costs." (Yes, that was May *1984*: these folks have been involved in selectronic for quite a while now!)

——————. "Yesterday's Wisdom, Tomorrow's Madness," *Direct* (April 1992), p. 74. "Using a predictive model to put the advertising message in the hands of just the right magazine reader is both possible and preferable... Stop spending good money on the worthless part of a publication's circulation when your message is meant for only 50%, 30% or maybe 10% of the readers."

—————— and Tom Collins. *The Great Marketing Turnaround: The Age of the Individual — and How to Profit From It.* Englewood Cliffs, New Jersey: Prentice-Hall, 1990. Hardcover, 336 pages. These guys are *really* good! Years ahead of others, they started to catalog the imaginative uses — first rare, then more common — of new data management and production technologies that allow direct marketers to address with greater and greater self-confidence the *individual* preferences of their customers. This book, and its predecessor before it (see below), set the tone and

· ·

established the vocabulary for marketers (including fundraisers!) to understand that "mass mail" — and mass marketing of all kinds — are truly a thing of the past.

————. *Maxi-Marketing*. The first of Rapp & Collins' two remarkable, trend-setting books on the *real* value of database information to marketers.

Shani, David, and Linda Reyer. "Videologs: Will They Replace Catalogs?", *Direct* (August 1990), p. 33. "Couple the right product with a clear objective, and this medium has been shown to work." The videocassettes' principal uses are to demonstrate the use of products, attract new customers and generate direct sales.

Sloane, Leonard. "Electronic 'Coupons': Savings but No Scissors," *New York Times* (April 21, 1990), p. 16. "Both shopper and producer are reaping benefits" from new point-of-purchase discounts at supermarkets, drugstores and other retail outlets. For the merchant, the "coupons" provide a mechanism "to track consumer purchases and to learn what is selling well and where and why." There are three major types: "post-purchase discounts" based on what the customer has bought or is expected to buy in the next visit, "pre-purchase discounts" from on-site machines that dispense coupons ("often by touching the screen on the dispensing machine"), and "frequent shopper programs" employing plastic ID cards that allow clerks to determine whether customers are eligible for either free merchandize or cash rebates at the register. How long can it be before such systems are available in our homes, via videophone, interactive TV or a home computer connected on-line to a shopping service?

Tedlow, Richard S. *New and Improved: The Story of Mass Marketing in America*. New York: Basic Books, Inc., 1990. Hardcover, 481 pages. Lest we leap to the conclusion that technology will dominate the society of the 21st century, it's important to remember the enormous role that marketing has played in changing, even creating consumer preferences — and in determining the fate of new, competing technologies. This book entertainingly tells the tale of some of the all-time great marketing wars in America — Coke vs. Pepsi, Ford vs. GM — and of the rise and fall of mercantile empires (Sears, Roebuck, A&P).

TECHNOLOGY AND THE FUTURE OF FUNDRAISING

Weiner, Allen. "Marketers Anxiously Await Interactivity's Promise," *Interactive World* (March, 1993), pp. 14-21. Weiner writes for and about the people who push American Express and Kool Aid; these people aren't thinking about high technology for its own sake — they want to know how they can use it to "move product" (see the next entry). The most imaginative of them can't wait for the "New Media" to become a reality, opening up hundreds of channels for information to flow between them and their customers. Why? Because savvy marketing and advertising people know what successful fundraisers and nonprofit executives are starting to learn, too: that marketing (or fundraising) is built on relationships with *individuals*. Weiner quotes one marketer: "'Having a [consumer's] name doesn't do anything for my clients... My client wants to zero in much more than that. What we need to do is figure out how to ask questions and start dialogues at a time the consumer is in the market to buy.'" Fundraisers and nonprofit managers please take note: the translation from the lingo of marketing and advertising isn't tough at all!

—————. "Moving Product Along the Interactive Highway," *Interactive World* (March 16, 1992), pp. 19-27. Catalogs some of the more imaginative uses marketers have made of 800- and 900-numbers, videotext services, interactive TV, and the like. For example, "In addition to making make, model and accessory information available on Prodigy, an on-line computer database subscription service, the Dearborn, Mich., Big Four carmaker offers consumers a PC-compatible diskette that provides detailed information on the 23 brands and 120 models in the Ford Motors family." Weiner cites statistics from Simmons Market Research Bureau indicating that, in 1983, 24.5% of the adult U.S. population (57 million people) shopped by mail or phone. In 1991, the percentage had risen to 52.6% (96 million people).

Technology in the business world

Andrews, Edmund L. "Cable TV Battling Phone Companies: 2 Technologies Vie to Control Future of Communication," *New York Times* (March 29, 1992), pp. 1, 16. This story, the basic facts of which are now familiar to most Americans, appeared nearly two years ago, when the facts

. . . .

weren't so familiar. It's a measure of how quickly change occurs in the world of technology that — already — many of the nation's biggest telephone companies are consuming the cable TV providers at a furious pace. (The proposed merger of Bell Atlantic and Tele-Communications, Inc., now pending, is only the tip of the iceberg.)

Brandt, Richard. "Boob Tube No More: The race is on to build digital TV converters — and some will lose," *Business Week* (June 7, 1993), pp. 100, 102. New business alliances are constantly forming and reforming, involving some of the world's richest corporations — and some of the most creative. The new digital cable converters, an essential element for inter-activity, will be selling to 4.5 million households annually by 1996; they'll cost $200 to $300 apiece. However, "It's unclear how the new converter boxes will be sold — and it could be years before agreed-upon standards appear." So don't hold your breath, waiting to talk back to Beavis and Butthead!

Bulkeley, William. "'Computerizing' Dull Meetings Is Touted As an Antidote to the Mouth That Bored," *Wall Street Journal* (November 28, 1992), pp. B1, B7. "Several studies seem to prove computerized meetings work much better." At Boeing, "total time involved in meetings was cut 71%. The calendar time required for team projects involving meetings was cut a whopping 91%... Nevertheless, with only an estimated 200 comput-erized rooms installed around the country, [IBM's] sales have 'been slower than expected.'"

Clark, Don. "New Vision of Communications: 'Data highways' lure billions in investment," *San Francisco Chronicle*, pp. B1, B6. The invest-ment needed to bring about the fabled "convergence" is staggering: "The Consumer Federation of America ... says studies show that rewiring the country for so-called broadband networks may require capital investment of $400 billion, or between $1,700 and $4,000 per user." This, by the way, is several times as much as the nation's gigantic interstate highway system cost when it was built in the 1950s (yes, taking inflation into account)!

——————. "Bay Area's State-of-the-Art Network," *San Francisco Chronicle*, pp. B1, B6. Pacific Bell is building BAGNet — Bay Area Gigabit Network — "to ring the bay, linking companies and research institutions from Berkeley to Palo Alto to Livermore... 'We're looking at on-line classrooms, information on demand for homes and businesses, houses that cry out when they are being robbed or are on fire.'"

Cringely, Robert X. "Welcome to the Future: Visionary Entrepreneurs Are Transforming the World and Creating a Flood of New Opportunities," *Success* (September 1992), pp. 22-28. The pseudonymous *Infoworld* computer industry gossip columnist focuses here on today's Steve Jobs and Bill Gates wanna-bes, including Adele Goldberg, Jaron Lanier and Ted Nelson. (The names may not mean much to you today; tomorrow, maybe they will!)

Davis, Stanley M. *Future Perfect*. Reading, Massachusetts: Addison-Wesley Publishing Company, 1987. Softcover, 243 pages. With chapter headings like "Any Time," "Any Place," No-Matter," "Mass Customizing," and "Hello from the Future," how could management consulting guru Tom Peters resist? He called this the "book of the decade." Davis writes: "[I]f you want to glimpse the shape of organizations in the future, look to the constraints of time, place and mass that are eased by technological developments. These enablements will be evident first in the products and services of the business, and in the processes used to produce them. Only later will they become evident in organization."

Doyle, Michael, and David Straus. *How to Make Meetings Work: The New Interaction Method*. New York: Jove Books, 1976. Softcover, 298 pages. This is one of the most widely recommended handbooks on its subject. I find it useful, especially as a reminder that, high tech or low tech, the means by which you keep a meeting on track must take into account the wishes (and foibles) of those who attend. In other words, people don't change much!

Dubashi, Jagannath, and Robert McGough. "A Wrenching Era of Change: Technology Takes Back Seat to Productivity," *San Francisco Examiner*, (February 9, 1992), p. E-14. "After years of spending 5 to 10 percent of sales on computerization with only a 1 percent gain in productivity to show for it, [business executives] are growing impatient with hardware 'solutions.'" An Electronic Data Systems executive says, "I don't think technology will dominate the industry so much in the years ahead, because the crucial issue for business is the utilization of that technology." The "service sector's technology paradox": using an index based at 100 in 1982, white-collar productivity had increased to 106.844 by 1990, while information technology capital per white-collar worker was at 203.555. And, to make matters worse, the productivity index was almost exactly as high in 1972 (having declined slightly through the 70s), while the capital investment index was only slightly above 50!

Feigenbaum, Edward, Pamela McCorduck and H. Penny Nii. *The Rise of the Expert Company: How Visionary Companies Are Using Artificial Intelligence to Achieve Higher Productivity and Profits.* New York: Vintage Books, 1988. Softcover, 321 pages. Tom Peters liked this one, too — and *this* time I see why. Combining solid, readable accounts of case studies with a lucid explanation of expert systems and their potential, these three pioneers in a field that is coming to be called "applied intelligence" (rather than "artificial intelligence") make a strong case about the practicality of expert systems in the here-and-now — in service organizations as well as manufacturing. Strongly recommended.

Garson, Barbara. *The Electronic Sweatshop: How Computers Are Transforming the Office of the Future Into the Factory of the Past.* New York: Penguin Books, 1988. Softcover, 288 pages. While just as negative as the subtitle implies, this artfully written little book is crammed with insight about how computers are *actually* used in many North American workplaces. The picture is not a pretty one, since the technology is principally used as an instrument of control — limiting the possibilities for human discretion for all but a tiny minority. Among those Garson studied: McDonald's frycooks; American Airlines reservations agents; Procter & Gamble word-processors; Shearson Lehman "brokers"; and social workers. It's all truly fascinating — but also truly overstated. Expert systems, for example, are summarily mischaracterized and dismissed as useful only as a mechanism to displace experienced workers.

Handy, Charles. *The Age of Unreason.* Boston: Harvard Business School Press, 1989. Hardcover, 278 pages. Tom Peters' name is on this dust-jacket, too. (That guy sure gets around!) But it's the venerable management guru, Warren Bennis, whose Foreword adorns this nifty little volume. Handy, better known in the United Kingdom than on these shores, also attracted the attention of *Business Week*, which kindly called him to my attention in a highly favorable review. Handy's "upside-down thinking" leads him to describe the emerging tripartite "shamrock" organization: one leaf, the shrinking "core," is populated by talented, dedicated professionals who work long hours for high wages, while a second leaf consists of independent contractors and the third, part-time workers — any of whom may be found virtually anywhere in the world, largely freed from traditional constraints of geography.

Howe, Kenneth. "Visa Banking on Debit Cards: Credit-card King Plots to Expand Plastic Empire," *San Francisco Chronicle* (March 16, 1992), pp. B1, B7. Owned by 22,000 banks, Visa has a big stake in the future of electronic banking — and they're just not going to take "no" as an answer from the American public. Sooner or later, these guys are going to figure out how to sell debit cards and start weaning us away from checks and from paper money. The implications for fundraisers are significant. In Canada, for example, Electronic Funds Transfer (EFT) programs have proven to be an unusually rich source of gifts for the nonprofit sector — and an ideal way to bond donors more tightly to the charities of their choice.

Johansen, Robert, et al. *Leading Business Teams: How Teams Can Use Technology and Group Process Tools to Enhance Performance*. Reading, Massachusetts: Addison-Wesley Publishing Company, 1991. Softcover, 216 pages. Like every product of writing by committee, this book has its faults: it's mechanistic, written without flair, and it contains too much mutually congratulatory back-slapping. But *Leading Business Teams* is a concise introduction to the fast-growing field of "groupware," which includes everything from easel-and-pad meeting facilitation to specially adapted computer networks to high-cost, computer-equipped meeting rooms crammed with lots of bells and whistles. And the authors are not glassy-eyed with approval of the technological tools; again and again, they emphasize that turning groups into teams is a process that involves human understanding and social skills.

....

Kleinfield, N. R. "Targeting the Grocery Shopper," *New York Times* (May 26, 1991), pp. 3-1, 3-6. "The laser scanner and the mag-striped card are altering grocery marketing." "For years, bar-code technology has been used to monitor supermarket inventories. Now it may also tell stores who is buying what."

Landler, Mark. "Media Mania: The Scramble for Digital Technology Is On. Here's a Cautionary View." *Business Week* (July 12, 1993), pp. 110-119. This article skillfully evaluates the contrasting strategies of some of the biggest players in the emerging world of interactivity: Time Warner, Tele-Communications, News Corp., Sony and Walt Disney. The essence of this report: "The true believers could win big — or lose their shirts." But one thing's for sure: some of them *will* lose.

McWilliams, Gary. "Ideas Galore, but Where Are the Goods?," *Business Week* (February 10, 1992), pp. 122-123. Hyped by Stewart Brand's fascinating book and its evangelistic director, Nicholas Negroponte, MIT's Media Lab has disappointed many of its corporate sponsors because patents — and marketable products — have been slow in coming.

Nasar, Sylvia. "Employment in Service Industry, Engine for Boom of 80's, Falters," *New York Times* (January 2, 1992), pp. A1, C5. "Except for health care, the services are in the throes of a pervasive shake-up very much like the one that racked smokestack manufacturing a decade ago." A slump in services productivity (possibly exaggerated because of poor statistics) "is partly a result of the huge influx of inexperienced workers in the 1970's and 80's. They also say service companies failed to use computers effectively... It is only now, when companies are under the gun, that they are really exploiting technology. While much of the hardware did not pay off in the past, managers are now learning to use it."

Quint, Michael. "Renewed Push for Pay-by-Phone," *New York Times* (March 7, 1992), pp. 18, 27. "Each check costs the bank and its customers about 79 cents; payments made electronically can cost as little as 25 cents... Even so, bill paying by telephone is used by only 4 percent or 5 percent of all households nationally, and is available to only about a third of the population..."

Ramirez, Anthony. "Video Meetings Get Cheaper, and a Bit Better," *New York Times* (February 5, 1992), p. C5. "Now $20,000 is a realistic starting point for executives willing to brainstorm in black and white."

Rheingold, Howard. "The Virtual Workgroup," *Publish* (April 1992), pp. 44-45. "As electronic mail and on-line communication services replace face-to-face meetings, your office environment will evolve in surprising ways." New technology "alters the way people think and work — almost always in unexpected ways." Rheingold cites the thinking of computer-age guru Douglas Engelbart, who predicted — in the 1960s — that changes in human relationships in the workgroup would prove to be the most explosive effects of the introduction of new technologies. For example, citing social psychologist Sara Kiesler, Rheingold says the intense use of E-mail and computer networking "'can break down hierarchical and departmental barriers, standard operating procedures, and organizational norms.'" The new technologies "make it possible for 'virtual task forces' to coalesce on the network, cutting across geographical and organizational boundaries to troubleshoot specific tasks."

Schrage, Michael. *Shared Minds: The New Technologies of Collaboration.* New York: Random House, 1990. Hardcover, 227 pages. The nationally syndicated columnist ("Innovation") writes with a sure hand and an encyclopedic command of his subject matter, which revolves around the concept of "computer-augmented meetings." But don't be turned off by this bloodless phrase. As Schrage writes, "Collaborative tools and documedia should add value to a collaboration, not merely reflect people's jottings or oral comments on-screen." In other words, this technology — like so many others — can change the character of human experience, in many ways for the better.

Sloane, Leonard. "Debit vs. Credit Cards: Pay Now, or Later," *New York Times* (March 21, 1992), p. 34. "'If only 5 percent of the transactions that involve the use of cash and checks migrates to debit cards, there will be more transactions than credit cards have... And that should happen by the end of this decade,'" said one banking industry observer. And a

....

MasterCard senior vice president added, "'The biggest change in banking in the 90's will be an extension of the A.T.M. for use as a debit card.'"

Strassman, Paul A. *Information Payoff: The Transformation of Work in the Electronic Age*. New York: The Free Press, 1985. Hardcover, 298 pages.

Wall Street Journal. "Technology," *The Wall Street Journal Reports* (April 6, 1992), pp. R1-R22. 15 articles by *Journal* staffers on some of the risks and the potential of emerging technologies — focusing, of course, on the implications for American business. Most intriguing to me was a piece entitled "Power Play" by G. Pascal Zachary, subheadlined, "Utilities see the 'intelligent' meter as the hub of a new two-way communications network. No wonder some cable-TV companies aren't happy." Turns out, in the town of Glasgow, Kentucky, pop. 12,000, the Electric Board, which buys its electricity from TVA, "decided it could save money by laying down cable next to the city's electric lines as part of a two-way communications network that would automatically reduce consumption at times of peak demand. Not long into the planning, however, the board's directors realized that the new system could double as a cable-TV network." So now it "offers cable service to about one-quarter of its electric customers for $13.50 a month... The utility's entry into the field prompted the existing cable provider to slash prices." And now the folks in Glasgow are "considering offering telephone service, too." Where might this lead? To "a 'media' utility, a sort of electronic highway that links residences with government, libraries and retailers."

Zuboff, Shoshana. *In the Age of the Smart Machine: The Future of Work and Power*. New York: Basic Books, Inc., 1988. Softcover, 468 pages. Management experts swear by this book, authored by one of the nation's leading academic experts in the study of technology's effects on people at work. I couldn't get through the book.

Social impact of emerging technologies

Abate, Tom. "Bay Area Cities Going On-Line: Computers, cable TV and high-tech phone systems keep government open 24 hours a day,"

San Francisco Examiner (November 7, 1993), pp. B-1, B-8. "The objective of all these technologies is to let citizens read city council agendas, order forms and transact ordinary government business after city offices have closed." The analogy: bank ATMs. Some projects involve significant public investments "like the state program that could spend $20 million over the next five years to put hundreds of kiosks in shopping centers and malls." (Through such kiosks, Californians will be able to renew their driver's licenses.)

Atchison, Sandra D. "Telecommuting: The Care and Feeding of Lone Eagles,'" *Business Week* (November 15, 1993), page 58. How towns such as Telluride, Colo., and Buffalo, Wyo., are exploiting technology to attract telecommuters. These New Age drifters are ideal newcomers: "'they bring their jobs with them.'"

Bleecker, Samuel E. "The Information Age Office," *The Futurist* (January-February 1991), pp. 18-20. "[T]he desk of the future will be a flat writing space with room underneath for a mobile file cabinet on wheels. When you arrive at work, you roll your personal file cabinet, filled with supplies and personal items, out of storage and slide it under a desk. You power up the built-in information appliance and insert your CD. It instructs the information appliance to route all your phone calls and other communications to this 'landing site.'"

Caruso, Denise, editor. "A Technology Policy for America: Six broad initiatives from Bill Clinton," *Digital Media: A Seybold Report* (January 18, 1993), pp. 9-12. *Digital Media* is a respected and widely read computer industry newsletter; in this issue, editor Denise Caruso reprinted verbatim the Clinton campaign's policy statement on technology, then devoted six pages to analyzing it. The six initiatives: "Building a 21st century technology infrastructure... Establishing education and training programs for a high-skill workforce... Investing in technology programs that empower America's small business... Increasing dramatically the percentage of federal R&D for critical technologies... Leveraging the existing federal investment in technology to maximize its contribution to industrial performance... Creating a world-class business environment for private sector investment and innovation." Caruso's take on all this: "We're ripe

••

for new infrastructure... We don't need to spend federal dollars... Civil liberties [considerations are a] gaping hole in the plan... Training programs don't address the central issue... Small businesses are the key to success." Her prescription includes focusing on standards, fostering competition, bearing down on the issue of data security and addressing the problem of "open access" versus "pay per view."

Gleick, James. "The Telephone Transformed — Into Almost Everything," *New York Times Magazine* (May 16, 1993), pp. 26 ff. "We're all connected by communications miracles. It's the people, still fumbling with the Switch Hook Flash, who are stuck in the Stone Age," writes the award-winning science writer, "Hold on, my other watch is ringing. The telephone is moving off the kitchen wall, onto the wrist and into the pocket."

Mander, Jerry, et al. "Questioning Technology," *Whole Earth Quarterly: Access to Tools & Ideas* (No. 73, December 21, 1991). The lion's share of this 144-page issue (edited by Howard Rheingold) is devoted to the impact of technology. It includes 20 articles and a much larger number of brief sidebars. While many of the pieces individually — and Rheingold's perspective comments — reflect a balanced point of view, much of this material is of the technology-is-death variety. If you're inclined to believe that change is bad for us all, you may enjoy reading it.

Lohr, Steve. "The New Technologies: Americans See Future and Say, 'So What?'", *New York Times* (October 7, 1993), pp. C1. A nationwide public opinion poll conducted in September 1993 for the Institute of Electrical and Electronics Engineers (IEEE) revealed that "only a small percentage of Americans think advanced electronics and computer developments will have a big impact on their lives during the next 10 years." ("People expected that the single largest effect on their lives... would be in health and medical care.") So what else is new? When did people stop hating to see things change?

Markoff, John. "A Digital Dilemma: In a World of Instant Copies, Who Pays for Original Work?", *New York Times* (August 9, 1992), page 4-18. "The problem of copyright infringement may hinder new technology," says the *Times'* technology reporter. Indeed, that problem — aggravated by the ease of copying not just paper but also computer disks, videotapes, even CD-ROMs — has been at the top of the agenda in many recent international trade negotiations. Publishers and Hollywood producers alike are wary, and rightfully so. As Denise Caruso is quoted as saying: "'[A] way has to be found to protect data if this revolution is going to be real."

—————. "Building the Electronic Superhighway: A key project of Clinton and Gore raises a debate: public or private?" *New York Times* (January 24, 1993), pp. 3-1, 3-6. Markoff zeroes in on one of this era's crucial public policy questions. Al Gore, who spearheads the Administration's technology policies, is at odds with many in private industry who want the Government out of the computer network business. In fact, the world's largest network, the Internet, was created by the U.S. Government — the Pentagon, in fact. The Internet now gives millions of users in more than 100 countries access to a vast wealth of information as well as a ready means of electronic (E-mail) communications.

Passell, Peter. "The Faxes Are Coming," *New York Times* (April 10, 1991), p. C2. "Suppose super-fast microprocessors, flat-panel high-definition television screens and fiber-optic cable made it practical to shop and perform most white-collar jobs by wire. The researchers estimate that some six million workers would abandon commuting, while 13 million business trips would be replaced with teleconferences each year. Householders would make three billion fewer shopping excursions; truck and airplane delivery miles would fall by 600 million annually." "If American homes are wired with fiber-optic cable anytime soon, many experts believe, the driving force will be video entertainment."

Postman, Neil. *Amusing Ourselves to Death: Public Discourse in the Age of Show Business.* New York: Penguin Books, 1985. Softcover, 184 pages.

—————. *Technopoly: The Surrender of Culture to Technology.* New York: Alfred A. Knopf, 1992. Hardcover, 222 pages. I couldn't get past page 66. This, Postman's 18th book, is sheer diatribe and, to my mind, lacks the grace and wit so often noted in his writing. The author's point of view is never in doubt, much less questioned; as he states in a brief introduction, "This book attempts to describe when, how, and why

....

technology became a particularly dangerous enemy." Postman's treatment ranges over the centuries — make that millennia — and spells out his feelings about all manner of technology, even going so far as to suggest that it's wise to question the utility of the written word, as a technological tool with negative as well as positive consequences. This book, then, is by no means just about computers; nonetheless, the core of Postman's argument seems to be on pp. 10-11: "to what extent has computer technology been an advantage to the masses of people? ... Their private matters have been made more accessible to powerful institutions. They are more easily tracked and controlled; are subjected to more examinations; are increasingly mystified by the decisions made about them; are often reduced to mere numerical objects. They are inundated by junk mail. They are easy targets for advertising agencies and political organizations. The schools teach their children to operate computerized systems instead of teaching things that are more valuable to children. In a word, almost nothing that they need happens to the losers. Which is why they are losers." Yuck! This guy is *never* going to be ready for the real world of the 21st Century!

Reich, Robert B. *The Work of Nations: Preparing Ourselves for 21st-Century Capitalism.* New York: Alfred A. Knopf, 1991. Hardcover, 331 pages. The influential Harvard economist and commentator, currently U.S. Secretary of Labor, describes the profound — and often disturbing — consequences of the globalization and growing technological complexity of American society: the increasingly bimodal distribution of income, with a small minority of "symbolic analysts" able to cope with technology reaping most of its rewards, while a large majority languishes in ever more dire poverty. Reich argues convincingly that the long-term best interest of the United States (or of any nation) in the world economy has much less to do with where goods are manufactured than with where they are conceived and designed — *where the greatest value is added.* A very important book.

Rheingold, Howard. "The Fable of the Pebble and the Pond," *Publish* (May 1992), pp. 38-40. The last of Rheingold's columns for this market-leading monthly circulated to desktop publishing professionals, it shows how a year and a half of thinking about the implications of our work with technology has tempered some of his earlier enthusiasm. Here's Rheingold's sober assessment of the future technology has in store for us: "Technologies that affect human thought and communication are at the center of the rapid changes taking place in the world's old economic, political, and social structures. Political and economic forces are also reacting to those changes through the way technologies are priced, regulated and marketed. Nobody really knows who will end up controlling and profiting from — and, conversely, who will be controlled by and pay for — the brave new world that our microchips and optical fibers are making possible. That's why an informed citizenry is crucial... Democracy doesn't just happen, and neither does prosperity."

Roszak, Theodore. *The Cult of Information: The Folklore of Computers and the True Art of Thinking.* New York: Pantheon Books, 1986. Softcover, 238 pages. Another anti-technology diatribe from an academic who's had more intelligent things to say about other subjects.

Sakaiya, Taichi. *The Knowledge-Value Revolution, or a History of the Future.* Tokyo: Kodansha International, 1991. Hardcover, 379 pages. *Now* I understand how the wisdom of the great sage now called Confucius in the West could seem so silly: it wasn't just bad translation — it was that *he wasn't writing for me!* This book, a runaway bestseller in Japan, prophesies "a new economic and social universe." But it paints a picture of that universe in such broad strokes that whatever insight the author might actually have is generally lost. Perhaps the cultural cues are all missing. However, Sakaiya does make one thing clear: like Reich (who wrote after him), he holds that the true value of goods produced in this post-industrial era lies not in their raw materials or the process by which they are manufactured but in their conception and design — their *knowledge-value.*

San Francisco Examiner. "Split the information superhighway," Editorial (November 14, 1993), page A-14. "It's not who owns the future electronic thoroughfare, but who controls the public's access to its 500-channel bandwidth." Regulators "shouldn't worry that firms building the electronic road will be too powerful, squeezing out traffic and driving up tolls. Instead, their concern ought to be providing open access... There's

....

an easy way to do this: Split the highway in two. Give half its 500-lane bandwidth to the road builder (it doesn't matter [who])... Keep the other 250 lanes as a common carrier." I was pleased to see this editorial recently, since it reflects my own feeling: I really *don't* care whether the Baby Bells beat out the cable TV people, or vice versa, or if they all eat each other for lunch. I just want to be sure I can get what I want and need from the emerging network without going broke in the process!

Schwartz, Evan I. "Putting the PC Into Politics: Partisans of 'Teledemocracy' Say It Will Energize the Electorate," *Business Week* (March 16, 1992), pp. 112-114. Some — with visions of "an electronic town meeting spanning the nation" — say that new technologies hold the promise of "a new type of participatory democracy." But this democracy is "not for everybody. 'How many poor people have Prodigy or CompuServe?" asks one futurist.

Snider, Jim, and Terra Ziporyn. *Future Shop: How Future Technologies Will Change the Way We Shop and What We Buy.* New York, NY: St. Martin's Press, 1992. Hardcover, 316 pages. The title is misleading — inexcusable, in my opinion, for a book written by consumer advocates — but, my annoyance notwithstanding, I found it both readable and interesting. The authors propose a dramatic innovation: government-certified "independent consumer information companies" that would draw information from a government-funded national consumer product information clearinghouse to serve the needs of individual consumers. Shopping consultants, in other words — replacing retail salespeople, the advertising industry, and much of the rest of our current economic infrastructure. All this, in response to the truly massive (read: unmanageable) amounts of information the authors expect to be available on the universal "omnimedia" network that subsumes what we now know as computers, telephones, and television. What about a similar "independent donor information service" for nonprofit organizations?

Sharrat, Bernard. "The Ancient Road to Hypertext: A scholar finds links between the Greek Sophists and today's information revolution," *New York Times Book Review* (November 28, 1993), page 2. Reviews *The Electronic Word: Democracy, Technology, and the Arts* by Richard A.

TECHNOLOGY AND THE FUTURE OF FUNDRAISING

Lanham (University of Chicago Press, 1993), which I wasn't able to find before going to press. The review includes this insight: "A proliferation of personalized multimedia productions may be no more socially enlightening than the provision of endless vacation videos has been." Sharrat also cites the following intriguing quote from Lanham's book: "For [today's university] students, life is not easy. They must learn three or four natural languages of God at least; they must learn a bureaucratized, difficult, highly Latinate language, rich in impersonal and hence guiltless passives, called 'soc-sci'; they must learn a mathematicized language, studded with charts and graphs, called "nat-sci"; and they must learn a computer language or two... Naturally enough, student-travelers wandering in this world often don't write very well, and sometimes indeed go crazy."

Spayd, Liz. "Papering the Walls — by the Box Full: Electronic Age Offers No Haven From Blizzard of Documents," *Washington Post* (November 14, 1993), pp. A1, A20. The use of paper continues to increase despite computers — in fact, I argue, *because* of computers. The long-standing vision of the "paperless office" has proven ephemeral. Now there are dozens of highly profitable companies that specialize in storing documents for paper-crazy businesses, government agencies — and nonprofit organizations.

Van Creveld, Martin. *Technology and War from 2000 B.C. to the Present.* New York: The Free Press, 1989. Hardcover, 342 pages.

Van, Jon. "End of the PC Era: Hardware Is Just Another Commodity; Future Lies in Chips and Software," *San Francisco Examiner* (November 24, 1991), p. E-14. "Some observers compare the American computer industry's current convulsions with the consolidation of automakers earlier in this century. Others suggest that the computer-makers' plight is considerably more severe...'What you see is the industry imploding on itself," said Paul Saffo, a research fellow at the Institute for the Future in Menlo Park, an academic think tank. 'The personal computer is a general-purpose device — a Swiss Army knife for office workers — and when it was introduced in 1980, it was proof that microprocessors had grown so cheap, everyone could afford to have one on a desktop. Now the PC has become a horseless carriage, a quaint reminder of the days when microprocessors were so expensive, you could only afford to have one." Saffo predicts workstations "far more powerful and widely connected than the machines now called workstations. These devices will be as easy to use as telephones and, like telephones, their utility will flow more from their network connections than from any computing horsepower under the hood of an individual unit." He also forecasts "information appliances, a broad selection of products combining intelligent chips with consumer electronics."

Networking

"Corporate Users Take Notes Seriously," *PC World* (January 1992), p. 60.

Andrews, Edmund L."Serving Workers on the Road with Data to Go," *New York Times* (January 8, 1992), p. C5. "Just as cellular telephone technology vaulted car telephones from rare curiosities to mass-market products, a new generation of [wireless] nationwide data networks is making it possible for both large and small companies to extend their office computer systems to employees on the road.""The new networks ... can also be used to let workers in the field retrieve almost any kind of data from computer data bases maintained thousands of miles away."

Bender, Eric. "Corporate Users Take Notes Seriously," *PC World* (January 1992), p. 60. Lotus' group communications package (sometimes called "groupware") is gaining a broad following and will be heavily promoted by the company in 1992.

Caruso, Denise. "The Future Is Interpersonal Computing," *San Francisco Examiner* (September 23, 1990), p. D-14. "The document of the 1990s is 'compound,' capable of incorporating many different types of digital data that can be used in many different ways. In Xerox's present strategy, this includes text and numbers and graphics. In the future, other types of data — including sound, video and animation — will be part of the document as well. A move in this direction is a leap toward real business productivity."

Cunningham, Scott, and Alan L. Porter. "Communication Networks: A Dozen Ways They'll Change Our Lives, *The Futurist* (January-

February 1992), pp. 19-22. "In the year 2000, fully 85% of American homes will subscribe to a cable service, and nearly 70% of those subscribing will have access to ISDN or two-way cable services." These "communication networks offer the promise of more-personalized media and widespread telecommuting, but they also threaten individual privacy and increase the potential for information discrimination."

Dertouzos, Michael L. et al. *Communications, Computers and Networks: How to Work, Play and Thrive in Cyberspace*. New York, NY: *Scientific American*, September 1991. Softcover, 138 pages. A remarkable, information-packed special issue of the venerable popularizer of trend-setting developments in science, with articles written by some of the seminal figures in the computer and communications industries. The essence of their message: "The transformation of civilization through the fusion of computing and communications technologies has been predicted for at least 50 years. Now the revolution has truly begun. The impact will be as profound as was the shift from an agrarian to an industrial society." The volume is extensively illustrated and contains many solid suggestions for further reading.

Erickson, Jim. "Info Highway Has Ruts, Detours: System could deliver quality information or 'garbage at the speed of light," *San Francisco Examiner* (November 7, 1993), page E-16. The public is responding unenthusiastically to high-tech services. For example, "In Cerritos in Southern California, GTE has been offering airline reservations, bill paying, stock quotes, business news, an encyclopedia, children's stories and games and other services in a pioneering interactive TV project. Out of 7.200 cable TV customers, only 350 people signed up for the two-way TV system, called Main Street."

Goodman, Ellen. "A Cautionary Tale," *San Francisco Chronicle* (October 21, 1993), page A25. "I haven't heard such hype about the future since the days when they were pushing fins on automobiles," the columnist writes. "They call the technology 'interactive' when in fact people will only interact with a TV screen and a remote control button."

Grimes, William. "Computer Networks Foster Cultural Chatting for Modem Times," *New York Times* (December 1, 1992), pp. B-1, B-4.

••

Well-known creative artists are going on-line to promote their wares —
and the on-line services that carry them. It's a "cultural explosion taking
place on computer information services around the clock, around the
world." Commercial services such as CompuServe, Prodigy, Genie and
America Online are actively involved.

Kapor, Mitchell, and Jerry Berman. "A Superhighway Through the
Wasteland?" *New York Times* Op-Ed (November 24, 1993), page A15. The
leaders of the Electronic Frontier Foundation, a nonprofit group that
promotes civil liberties in digital media, argue that "the [information]
superhighway should be required to provide so-called open platform
services [so that] every person would have access to the entire superhighway... [C]ompanies controlling the superhighway must be required to carry
other programmers' content, just as phone companies must provide service
to anyone who is willing to pay for it." They add, "Americans will come to
depend on the superhighway even more than they need the telephone."
The solution? New laws for communications technology by amending the
Communications Act of 1934.

Lohr, Steve. "Who Will Control the Digital Flow? A traffic report
for the data superhighway", *New York Times* (October 17, 1993), pp. 4-1,
4-3. There are two models the Information Highway might follow: "In the
broadcast model... entertainment would be the driving force, leading to
what has been called the 500-channel future." But, argues Lotus Development Corp. founder Mitchell Kapor, "'We don't want to build an information
infrastructure that is eight lanes one way and a footpath the other way.'
Mr. Kapor would rather see the highway modeled along the lines of the
Internet... On the Net... anyone with a personal computer and a modem
can send and receive information to anyone else... This diverse, egalitarian
nature is what advocates like Mr. Kapor want preserved in the 'rules of the
road.'"

Markoff, John. "New Coalition to Seek a Public Data Highway,"
New York Times (October 26, 1993), page C2. "Seeking to insure that the
national data highway is not strictly a big-business affair, a coalition of
more than 60 nonprofit, consumer, labor and civil rights groups" formed
an organization to broaden public discussion of the technology: the

Telecommunications Policy Roundtable. This is an effort by public interest organizations to avoid being locked out of the gathering debate about the growing "Information Superhighway."

————————. "Traffic Jams Already on the Information Highway," *New York Times* (November 3, 1993), pp. A1, C7. The volume of traffic on the Internet is growing at such a furious pace that "'It's just like when everybody flocks to a beach on a Sunday,'" Markoff quotes a computer scientist as saying. "'You sit in the car and wait and wait and wait.'" The growth rates are staggering: for one service, from 100,000 queries in June to 400,000 in October; for use of one information retrieval program, a 400 percent increase in 1993 alone.

Perratore, Ed. "Networking CD-ROMs: The Power of Shared Access," *PC Magazine* (December 31, 1991), pp. 333-363. "For access to large amounts of data, CD-ROMS can't be beat. And to provide that information to the most people at the lowest cost, CD-ROMs belong on the network — especially now that most CD-ROM software companies have lifted their archaic licensing restrictions." This article evaluates five alternative CD-ROM networking systems.

Rheingold, Howard. *The Virtual Community: Homesteading on the Electronic Frontier.* Reading, Massachusetts: Addison-Wesley Publishing Company, 1993. Hardcover, 288 pages. A later and more down-to-earth effort by the author of the popular book, *Virtual Reality* (see the section below entitled, "Bells, whistles and breakthroughs"). Rheingold skillfully traces the history and the implications of the mushrooming electronic networks collectively called the "Information Highway." He speaks whereof he knows: for years, he's lived a dual life, respectable magazine editor and freelance book writer by day, denizen of fantasy worlds without number by night — accessed through The Well, a Sausalito, Calif.-based computer network. Rheingold has a balanced view of the new technology's potential: he obviously likes the stuff, and sees the good that it can do, but technology's potential to stifle the human spirit and constrain our freedoms troubles him, too. This is a very important book — must reading for anyone eager to join in the debate over the future of the Net.

....

Schrage, Michael. "Innovation: High tech ignores 'gray market,'" *San Francisco Examiner* (November 7, 1993), page E-16. "A large and relentlessly growing chunk of the 60-plus population now has the leisure, the discretionary income and — contrary to its media image as a bunch of hapless technophobes — the willingness to integrate computing into everyday life." America Online president Steve Case acknowledges, "'[I]t turns out that older people make excellent customers for us. They have lots of time, a lot of them now use computers to track their investments, and more of them are interested in using electronic mail to communicate with their grandchildren.'" Fundraisers, take note!

Templeton, Brad. "Kapor Praises ISDN as Key to Future," *Bay Area Computer Currents* (February 11-24, 1992), p. 42. Mitch Kapor, who founded Lotus Development and, after bailing out of Lotus, the Electronic Frontier Foundation, asserts that ISDN connections using ordinary copper telephone lines is "the key to universal access to the network world." Fiber optic lines, while far superior, aren't really essential, Kapor said.

Therrien, Lois, and Chuck Hawkins. 'Wireless Nets Aren't Just for Big Fish Anymore," *Business Week* (March 9, 1992), pp. 84-85. "The telecom giants aim to sell mail and data services to the masses" through wireless data networks, fleet dispatch systems, cellular phone networks and advanced paging devices.

The coming convergence

Andrews, Edmund L. "F.C.C. Clearing Airwaves for an Era Without Wires," *New York Times* (September 20, 1993), pp. 1, C10. "On Thursday, after four years of work, the Federal Communications Commission will adopt rules that will create three to six new wireless networks in every city and town. Bringing stiff new competition and probably a steep plunge in prices, these services are expected to reach millions of new customers and could eventually replace phones anchored by copper wires... The new 'personal communications services' will be capable of sending data, images and perhaps even video to an expanding family of nomadic computing devices...Arthur D. Little... has estimated that personal communications services will generate 60 million customers in the United

States by 2005." In other words, in barely more than a decade, your donors, and mine, will be carrying their phones around in their pockets — and receiving appeals and live messages by fax and video even when they're on the run. They'll be getting them from ... someone. Will you and I be sending them?

Auletta, Ken. "Annals of Communications: Barry Diller's Search for the Future," *The New Yorker* (February 22, 1993), pp. 49-61."Diller's new venture began with a laptop and a home-shopping cable network — and it stunned Hollywood. But it may make him billions." One of the nation's most successful business reporters tackles one of America's most celebrated media moguls: the man who built the Fax TV network from scratch, then left and, eventually, hooked up with the QVC Network, a little-regarded home shopping enterprise. As Auletta details, Diller had bigger things in mind from the start — and it was mere months before Diller patched together an audacious bid for Paramount Communications, one of the country's top movie production studies. At this writing, Diller's mano-a-mano contest with billionaire MTV-owner Sumner Redstone for control of Paramount is unresolved; but the story, a colorful one to be sure, is instructive for its own sake, regardless of the outcome. The continuing tussle for control of the Network will attract society's boldest, and not always most attractive, figures: we can expect to be entertained, then, even if the way things turns out isn't to our liking.

Burka, Karen. "The Telephone in Your Future: High-Tech Mix'n Match," *Direct* (February 1992), pp. 30-32. "Hybrid campaigns that integrate different telemarketing technologies, such as live and automated operators, 800 and 900 numbers, are gaining in popularity among direct marketers."

Carmody, Deirdre. "The Media Business: Time's Chief Sees Need for Magazines to Evolve," *New York Times* (October 12, 1993), page C13. "Many leading magazine companies are establishing divisions to explore how the franchises of their magazines can be expanded by the new technology, which includes on-line services; CD-ROM's...; and an ever-increasing number of cable channels. Despite his emphasis on this new

· ·

technology, [*Time*'s editor] reiterated his company's commitment to continue publishing its own magazines."

Farhi, Paul. "Fighting for a Leading Edge on the Future: Cable TV, Phone Firms Compete for Control of Tomorrow's Technology," *Washington Post* (January 24, 1992), pp. 1, 14. The cable TV industry is exercising considerable political muscle in Washington to beat the Regional Bell Operating Companies in the race to dominate the information channels of the future. But it appears increasingly likely that neither industry will win the race: joint ventures may dominate the entertainment and information markets of the 21st century.

—————. "Waves of the Future: FCC Chairman Alfred Sikes Has Visions of a Technological Revolution," *Washington Post* (May 5, 1991), pp. H1, H4. Al Sikes believes "We're moving from the age of information to the age of knowledge." Farhi writes, "His primary objective: to erode regulatory barriers that keep those in one portion of the telecommunications industry protected from competing with those in other parts. He envisions an era of truly open markets, in which telephone companies offer television programs, and cable companies hawk services now provided by phone companies."

Freiberger, Paul. "Shaken to the Core: Apple Computer's Tumultuous Year Will Shape it for a Decade," *San Francisco Examiner* (January 12, 1992), pp. E-1, E-9. A computer industry observer is quoted as saying, "The future is increasingly going to be appliance-like devices. Apple's emphasis on software positions it to deliver those things." So does its alliance with Sony, which will manufacture the hardware for many new Apple products.

Glaberson, William. "Creating Electronic Editions, Newspapers Try New Roles," *New York Times* (August 16, 1993), pp. 1, C6. "[E]lectronic newspapers are finally arriving on personal computer screens across the country,..'Our mail goal,'" says one newspaper executive, "'is to make the newspaper itself more valuable to people.'" Fundraisers could do worse to look at their own appeals in this same light!

Glenn, Jerome C. "Conscious Technology: The Co-evolution of Mind and Machine," *The Futurist* (September-October 1989), pp. 15-20.

"The Post-Information Age will see the merger of humans and their technologies, perhaps creating an entirely new species."

Gore, Albert, Jr. "Information Superhighways: The Next Information Revolution," *The Futurist* (January-February 1991), pp. 21-23. The Vice President has long been touting the economic virtues of investment in high-tech research and development, beginning with his years in the U.S. Congress and continuing through his service in the Senate. "A network of 'information superhighways' would help turn the mounting load of unused data into knowledge for problem-solving."

Jones, Terril. "France Loves its Telephone Computer: User-friendly System Offers Amazing Variety of Services," *San Francisco Examiner* (November 24, 1991), p. E-14. "The Minitel computer has gone far beyond its early use as a phone book and electronic singles bar in the decade since the government, as a gift, began connecting millions of them to home and business telephones. Users in France and its overseas territories can plug into the system to buy furniture, transfer money between bank accounts and check airline or train schedules, weather, the stock market and soccer scores... A user taps out the name of the desired service, following simple directions on the screen, without having to learn computer programs or terminology. Services cost by the minute. Minitel, now connected to 20 percent of French telephone lines and expanding to other continents, offers 16,000 of them."

Ramirez, Anthony. "Bell Atlantic Plans Service That Links Phone Numbers," *New York Times* (March 17, 1992), pp". C1, C5. A new, $15-25 per month, "one person, one number" service will allow customers to receive calls at the office or at home; on a cellular telephone, a fax machine or a pager; or by a message left on voice-mail. Callers will dial a single number and reach a menu of choices ("1 at home, 2 at the office, 3 by fax," etc.)

Schwartz, John. "The Next Revolution," *Newsweek* (April 6, 1992), pp. 42-48. "A marriage of computers and electronics will spawn everything from smart TVs to portable secretaries — and change how you live and work." Schwartz mentions "TV systems that help cull good shows from the growing morass of cable trash" — just one example of how, finally,

....

information management technologies will allow us to "take the fire hose of information and draw off eight-ounce glasses at will." Another example: "Apple has a program that could be released as early as next year, code-named Rosebud, which combs on-line news wire services for stories users care about — without having to learn the arcane commands used by most services today. It can put together a newspaper from many topics or take individual requests."

Shao, Maria. "Baby Bells Prepare to Ring in Information Age: PacTel and Others Testing Electronic Publishing Waters," *San Francisco Examiner* (January 12, 1992), pp. E-1, E-4. A "videophone" that looks like a laptop computer and responds to voice commands will permit callers to call up flight schedules, book tickets, even select seats from diagrams onscreen — and to purchase all manner of other goods and services from choices available through an electronic version of the Yellow Pages. The same videophone will offer sports and entertainment information — and two-way voice-and-picture communications. All this is described in a demonstration video from the Pacific Telesis Group.

Siegmann, Ken. "Personal Communicator Is a High-Tech Magic Act," *San Francisco Chronicle* (November 29, 1991), pp. D1, D3. "Imagine a doctor making his hospital rounds. He walks into a patient's room, and pulls out a small device, about the size of a checkbook. He opens it up to see a computer screen and a few buttons. He taps on the screen with his pen and writes the patient's name. The device makes a wireless connection to the hospital's computer, and displays the patient's chart. He taps on the screen again and checks the inventory in the hospital pharmacy, makes a selection and signs his name on the screen. The pharmacy then delivers the prescribed drugs to the patient's room. No such device is on the market today, but it's not far off. General Magic Inc., a Mountain View [Calif.]-based startup company that's financed by some of the most influential players in the computer industry, is secretly working on what its founders have called a 'personal intelligent communicator.'"

Weinstein, Stephen B., and Paul W. Shumate. "Beyond the Telephone: New Ways to Communicate," *The Futurist* (November-December 1989), pp. 8-12. "Telephone networks will increasingly expand their capacity with fiber optics and broadband. Instead of just phoning home, you'll be able to send pictures, texts, data, and even video... Fiber to all subscribers is a virtual certainty in 25-30 years, and many subscribers are likely to have it in the 1990s."

Video and multimedia

Andrews, Edmund L."Pursuing Al Sikes's Grand Agenda," *New York Times* (June 2, 1991), pp. 3-1, 3-6. FCC Chairman Alfred C. Sikes is bent on freeing up space on the radio spectrum for advanced new services, including mobile satellite services, radio-based pocket-sized telephones and radio links for personal computers.

———————. "FCC Plan to Set Up 2-Way TV: A Special Frequency for Ordering Goods," *New York Times* (January 11, 1992), pp. D1, D5. An FCC proposal to set aside a special frequency for ordering goods and services through television sets "indicates that the agency now believes the technology for two-way interactive television has advanced to the point where it is ready for commercial use."

———————. "The Lure of Digital Television," *New York Times* (June 24, 1990), p. F9. "The union of high-definition television and computers now seems more likely."

Bove, Tony, and Cheryl Rhodes. "Will the Real Multimedia Please Stand Up?," *Desktop* (Vol IV, No. 1), pp. 37-40. "There's QuickTime, MPC, IBM's Ultimedia, not to mention CDTV and CD-I — this multi-confusing assortment of technologies leaves users with multiple choices" — and massive confusion, which will surely (if temporarily) retard the growth of this exciting new field.

Christian Science Monitor. "Viewer Control — Cable TV's Next Revolution: Folks at Home Tell Stations What to Send — and When," *San Francisco Chronicle* (May 24, 1991), page 1. 450 south Denver homes are the site of "the most comprehensive test yet of viewer-controlled cable television," including "video on demand." The test is a joint venture of Tele-Communications Inc., US West and AT&T.

· ·

Clark, Don. "Pixar and Disney Make Animators More Productive," *San Francisco Chronicle* (March 12, 1992). The unabridged "Oxford English Dictionary will come out on CD-ROM in June for $895 — one-third the price in standard book form." And CD-ROM permits users to search material in ways that are difficult, even impractical in paper volumes. Yet only 3 percent of PCs now in use are equipped with CD-ROM drives, so "the industry could use the equivalent of a Sony Walkman" ... and Sony's introducing it later this year for an initial price of around $1,000. (It's the CD-ROM XA, nicknamed Bookman, an improved version of the limited-utility Sony Data Discman.)

Naver, Michael. "Making Multimedia," *CompuServe Magazine* (January 1992), pp. 10-17. "'Picture a large screen on your desk showing three colleagues in different cities, plus the logo of a newsletter you're all working on interactively,' Naver quotes an Intel executive as saying. 'Real-time conferencing allows you to open those four windows, and all of you can modify the logo.'"

Pollack, Andrew. "New Interactive TV Threatens the Bliss of Couch Potatoes," *New York Times* (June 18, 1990), pp. 1, D9. Video games have helped conditioned Americans to the potential of interactive TV services. But, so far, "the only interactivity that appears to be developing into a successful business is the simplest approach, requiring no special equipment in homes." This approach uses 800- and 900-numbers.

Rash, Wayne, Jr. "Multimedia Moves Beyond the Hype," *Byte* (February 1992), pp. 85-88. "Products finally arrive that solve real business problems" in creating presentations, training and educational materials.

Schwartz, Evan I. "Multimedia Is Here, and it's Amazing," *Business Week* (December 16, 1991), pp. 130-131. The "bottom line" from the people who may lay claim to inventing that overworked phrase? "You may want to see how it all shakes out before you count yourself among the first buyers of these relatively pricey setups."

TECHNOLOGY AND THE FUTURE OF FUNDRAISING

Trends and trend-meisters

Cetron, Marvin, and Owen Davies. *American Renaissance: Our Life at the Turn of the 21st Century.* New York: St. Martin's Press, 1989. Hardcover, 400 pages. A prolific futurist's rose-colored view of early 21st-century America: a multiracial society enjoying a life of leisure, free of AIDS and supreme in the world economy. "If we summon the needed vision and spirit, human beings will soon be on their way to an emancipation like nothing since Abraham Lincoln. Intelligent machines will carry out most of the drudgery that now claims our lives, while we will be free to create — art, science, and new goods and services — as only human beings (now) can."

Cringely, Robert X. *Accidental Empires: How the Boys of Silicon Valley Make Their Millions, Battle Foreign Competition, and Still Can't Get a Date.* Reading, Massachusetts: Addison-Wesley Publishing Company, Inc., 1992. Hardcover, 324 pages. Though the focus of this entertaining book is squarely on the personalities — foibles, mostly — of the aforementioned "boys of Silicon Valley," the pseudonymous Cringely, *Infoworld's* gossip columnist, is knowledgeable and insightful. He doesn't lose sight of the big picture. "It takes society thirty years, more or less, to absorb a new information technology into daily life. It took about that long to turn movable type into books in the fifteenth century. Telephones were invented in the 1870s but did not change our lives until the 1900s. Motion pictures were born in the 1890s but became an important industry in the 1920s. Television, invented in the mid-1920s, took until the mid-1950s to bind us to our sofas." In 1992, we are "about halfway down the road to personal computers' being a part of most people's everyday lives." But it's not yet clear *how* computers will change our lives. "Radio was invented with the original idea that it would replace telephones and give us wireless communications. That implies two-way communication, yet how many of us own radio transmitters? ... Television ... was envisioned at first as a two-way visual communication medium. Early phonographs could record as well as play and were supposed to make recordings that would be sent through the mail, replacing written letters. The magnetic tape cassette was invented by Phillips for dictation machines, but we use it to hear music on Sony Walkmans. Telephones went the other direction, since Alexander Graham Bell first envisioned his invention being used to pipe music to remote groups of people."

Diebold, John. *The Innovators: The Discoveries, Inventions, and Breakthroughs of Our Time.* New York: Truman Talley Books/Plume, 1990. Softcover, 303 pages. Apparently, someone heavily edited this guy's first book, *Automation*, which was first published in 1952 and caused a stir for years. This book is almost unreadable.

Dychtwald, Ken, Ph.D., and Joe Flower. *Age Wave: The Challenges and Opportunities of an Aging America.* Los Angeles: Jeremy P. Tarcher, Inc., 1989. Hardcover, 380 pages.

Edwards, Lynda. "Trend Tyranny: Inside the World of Professional Trend Spotters — the People Whom Big Corporations Pay Millions to Predict What You'll be Wearing, Eating and Thinking a Year From Now," *This World* (March 17, 1991), pp. 8-11. A wide-eyed *Spy* magazine article revealing more than most of us care to know about Faith Popcorn and her fellow trend-mavens, with a cursory look at the "Trends of the '90s." (Hint: they all have cutesy names, few of which are intelligible to those of us who don't watch sitcoms.)

Hafner, Katie, and John Markoff. *Cyberpunk: Outlaws and Hackers on the Computer Frontier.* New York: Simon and Shuster, 1991. Hardcover, 368 pages. This story quickly loses its charm as, in the opening chapters, it becomes so very clear how utterly unattractive are the protagonists. The object lesson to be drawn from these three long tales of "outlaws and hackers" is that, like any tool or technique, the computer can become an object of unreasonable veneration for those who lack the social skills to form rewarding personal relationships with other people. Reading about Kevin Mitnick, the hacker-outlaw-loser profiled in the opening section, I kept wondering what had happened to him so that he never developed a *life*.

Markoff, John. "Denser, Faster, Cheaper: The Microchip in the 21st Century," *New York Times* (December 29, 1991), p. 5. "Moore's Law," postulated in the 1960s by Intel confounder Gordon Moore, predicted that "chip density, or capacity, would double every two years. In 1976, he revised his 'law' to state that chip density would double every year and a half." And so far he's been right. "By the end of the decade, schoolchildren will be playing with video-game equipment and other machines as powerful as today's supercomputers. And scientists and engineers will be exploring a range of commercial and research applications for artificial intelligence, machine vision and voice recognition."

McLuhan, Marshall. *The Gutenberg Galaxy.* New York: The New American Library, 1962. Softcover, 350 pages.

——————- and Quentin Fiore. *The Medium is the Massage: An Inventory of Effects.* New York: Bantam Books, 1967. Softcover, 159 pages.

Naisbitt, John. *Megatrends: Ten New Directions Transforming Our Lives.* New York: Warner Books, 1982. Hardcover, 290 pages. Here's Naisbitt's table of contents: "(1) Industrial Society —— Information Society. (2) Forced Technology —— High Tech/High Touch. (3) National Economy —— World Economy. (4) Short Term —— Long Term. (5) Centralization —— Decentralization. (6) Institutional Help —— Self-Help. (7) Representative Democracy —— Participatory Democracy. (8) Hierarchies —— Networking. (9) North —— South. (10) Either/Or —— Multiple Option." Now you know all you need to know!

Pollack, Andrew. "Two Men, Two Visions of One Computer World, Indivisible: An 'Open Hyperdocument System' — or Xanadu," *New York Times* (December 8, 1991), p. 13. Two men who just won't quit: Doug Engelbart, who, in the 1960s, "invented the computer mouse, on-screen windows and several other techniques that are only now coming into widespread use," and Ted Nelson, another computer visionary who has been pursuing the concept of "hypertext" since 1961. Hypertext — conceived by Engelbart at Stanford Research Institute — "can be envisioned as data arranged on imaginary notecards. The reader jumps from card to card, choosing his or her own path through the material." Nelson's hypertext application, Xanadu, "will be a database program to help people work together and keep track of documents. For example, an architect might be able to point to a spot on a blueprint and immediately jump to a memo explaining the reasons behind that part of the design." Engelbart,

•••

who "wants to help organizations make faster and better decisions," is working essentially alone on a similar vision.

Popcorn, Faith. *The Popcorn Report: Faith Popcorn on the Future of Your Company, Your World, Your Life.* New York: Doubleday, 1991. Hardcover, 226 pages. I expected to leaf through this book with a sneer on my lips but instead found myself reading with interest. Though Popcorn's "10 Trends" obviously derive much more from her own intuitive abilities than from the idiosyncratic "method" she describes, they're shot through with genuine understanding and insight. The Fortune 500 companies that pay her megabucks to help them make positioning and marketing choices appear to be getting their money's worth. Here, for example, is one passage that incorporates Popcorn's views on a number of crucial current trends in American business: "every community could have its own neighborhood office center complete with its own 'watercooler,' offering large-scale office services and supplies (you'll charge these to your company) in a clublike setting. The corporations will monitor their employees the same way they do now, by measuring their productivity,. As for non-corporate entrepreneurs: small, local businesses will rise up to provide collateral services. Niche businesses will move physically closer to their niche markets." (pp. 52-53) For-profits and nonprofits alike can learn a lot by pondering that vision of the near future!

Toffler, Alvin. *Power Shift: Knowledge, Wealth and Violence at the Edge of the 21st Century.* New York: Bantam Books, 1990. Softcover, 611 pages.

—————. *The Third Wave.* New York: Bantam Books, 1980. Softcover, 537 pages.

—————. *Future Shock.* New York: Bantam Books, 1970. Softcover, 561 pages. Though breathless and often confusing trivia with truly significant matters, Toffler's now-classic look at the direct, personal *impact* of new technologies is still remarkable in its central perception: that the pace of change may be as profound as change itself.

TECHNOLOGY AND THE FUTURE OF FUNDRAISING

Bells, whistles and breakthroughs

Bove, Tony. "Voyager's Expanded Books: Even Better Than the Real Thing?", *Bay Area Computer Currents* (February 11-24, 1992), p. 35. Using standard diskettes (not CD-ROM) on Macintosh PowerBook laptop computers, the Voyager Company's $20 Expanded Books "let you search the text for specific words or phrases. You can type the words, or select them with the mouse and use a pop-up menu of search choices. The electronic books also let you mark pages so that you can go back to them quickly, and type annotations in the margins of pages. You can also copy text into a notes file."

Brand, Stewart. *The Media Lab: Inventing the Future at MIT*. New York: Penguin Books, 1987. Softcover, 285 pages. A spirited and thought-provoking look at the long-term implications of the new technologies of telecommunications, written by the celebrated founder of the *Whole Earth Catalog*. Wide-ranging, imaginative and entertaining; essential for understanding of this subject. An illuminating introduction for the general reader to many of the terms and concepts central to understanding the new technologies of telecommunications: "fiber optics," "bandwidth," "information density," "ISDN."

Davis, Susan. "A Book Revolution: 'Electronic Books,' the Wave of the Future, Melding TV Medium with Library Reference Stacks," *San Francisco Examiner* (September 17, 1989), p. D-3. "The idea is not new. Hidden words unfold behind mirrors or doors, scenes come alive, characters follow their own wills. It's the stuff of children's stories... [but now] it's for real." For example, the "Electric Cadaver" developed at Stanford teaches human anatomy to medical students. "A student might start, for instance, with a detailed drawing of the skeletal system, move to more detailed drawings of the skull and facial structure, rotate them, watch an animation of tooth growth, listen to vocal chord sounds, and then switch to digitized photos of a cadaver's nasal cartilage. With each 'jump,' students have access to text explaining how different parts work. The linking activity itself helps students understand how the parts work together."

Dvorak, John C. "Inside Track," *PC Magazine* (March 31, 1992), p. 95. A new CD-ROM just introduced to the market: "Monarch Notes on CD-ROM." It's got 'em all, including many that have long been out of print. And the total price is $99. The cost of cramming just took a nosedive!

Egol, Len. "Neural Networks Add 'Brainpower to Data," *Direct* (February 1992), p. 17. A neural network — "a computerized statistical technique ... that calculates weights for predictable customer behavior characteristics such as age, income, education, time on the job, etc." — can become an invaluable marketing tool because it "can outdo humans in handling complex data relationships." Neural networks can "measure risk, forecast response and sales, predict cancellations and renewals, monitor business and customer trends, develop cross-sell profiles, and automate such tasks as processing an insurance application."

Epstein, Robert. "A New Era in Home-Entertainment Gadgetry," *San Francisco Chronicle* (January 7, 1992), p. E3. They're costly — upwards of $10,000 — but "a new crop of home-bound products has dared to enter the marketplace, challenging how we spend our entertainment dollars, offering products that have the potential of turning living rooms into theaters and homes into virtual entertainment multiplexes."

Feder, Barnaby J. "For Bar Codes, an Added Dimension," *New York Times* (April 24, 1991), pp. C1, C7. New types of barcodes, which "allow lines of code to be stacked up, storing information in two dimensions instead of in one line," ... "are expected to replace lengthy typewritten shipping documents, allow manufacturers to individually label small items like microchips, and help prevent the mishandling of hazardous waste, among other applications."

Fox, Steve. "Adobe's Master Document," *PC World* (January 1992), p. 16. One of the barriers to free and easy use of computers is about to fall with the advent of a new product from Adobe, creator of the "PostScript" language that allows laser printers to produce a multiplicity of typefaces with complete consistency. Now, with Carousel, any document — whether created in DOS, Windows, UNIX, or OS/2 or on a Macintosh or NeXT computer — may be shared with another PC regardless of how it was manufactured ... so long as it's equipped with Carousel. All of a sudden, PCs will actually be able to talk with one another!

Gelernter, David. *Mirror Worlds, or: The Day Software Puts the Universe in a Shoebox ... How It Will Happen and What It Will Mean.* New York: Oxford University Press, 1991. Hardcover, 237 pages. A Yale computer science professor with a wacky sense of humor and a love of the vernacular tells an entertaining and provocative — if not always easily understandable — tale of the software marvels in our collective future. These are the large-scale computer models, or "Mirror Worlds," in which computers will track and measure significant changes in some of the most massive human and natural systems, providing those with the requisite skills an infinite number of windows onto reality. Gelernter is overly fond of metaphors, and mixes them liberally, and occasionally to the point of incomprehensibility. (Sample: "A dollhouse is a nest of tuple spaces. The front lobby is the outer tuple space; the rooms it contains are also tuple spaces, nested inside the outer one, and so on. Each televiewer is an infomachine plus a tuple. (The tuple is the 'screen' and the infomachine is the stuff inside the TV set, so to speak: The infomachine keeps the tuple up-to-date.) The blackboards floating around inside each room are tuples.") Despite such silliness, however, the book is rewarding, and it may prove to be important, because, at base, it describes the author's informed view of the *structures* through which we will access information on the emerging world database. Heady stuff, this!

Haavind, Robert. "Hypertext: The Smart Tool for Information Overload," *Technology Review* (November-December 1990), pp. 43-50. "Emerging methods for finding, exchanging and filtering information promise a new era in computer use." "The power of hypertext unfolds in [a] hypothetical treatment of Hamlet... The play's script is laced with linkages to information on unfamiliar terms and references as well as background material on Shakespeare and his Globe Theater. An inquiry on the protagonist's state of mind might lead to text by Freud on dreams." "Hypertext pioneer Douglas Engelbart, now at Stanford University, is spearheading an organization called the Bootstrap Community to promote ... interchangeability among hypertext, hypermedia, and groupware documents."

....

Hall, Trish. "'Virtual Reality' Takes Its Place in the Real World," *New York Times* (July 8, 1990), pp. 1, 12. Virtual reality "can enable surgeons to use scalpels without drawing blood and colleagues separated by thousands of miles to work in the same space."

Henderson, Khali. "Future of Fax: Dynamic and Graphic," *4th Media Journal* (July 1991), pp. 57-60. Interactive fax technology is "on a pathway to becoming a $2 billion a year industry." It's now possible "to send images, including halftone illustrations, photographs and even video over the fax machine."

Holusha, John. "Adding Lanes to Data Highways: Project Seeks Wider Use of Fiber Optics," *New York Times* (July 24, 1991), pp. C1, C7. "8-foot-high Video Windows that virtually bring ... distant groups into the same room are a product of a new technology intended to expand drastically the amount of data that optical fibers can carry." [And "virtual audio" can create the illusion that voices are coming from different locations in the scene depicted on-screen.]

Jones, Alex S. "Small Fax Newspaper Sees a Way to Big Profits," *New York Times* (August 12, 1991), "In two small Illinois towns, a one-page fax newspaper called Fax Today has challenged the local daily with some success, prompting predictions that similar fax papers could spread like a virus across the country and pose a threat to newspapers."

Kaplan, Alan. *"Manager's Guide to the New Software: Object-Oriented Programs Are Making Applications More Powerful and Less Complex," PC World* (January 1992), pp. 228-233. "Object Linking and Embedding" and "Dynamic Data Exchange," which permit the free exchange and simultaneous updating of data and images among different software programs, are becoming more widespread. This permits some non-technical computer users to handle software in ways that are easier, more natural and more suitable to them individually.

Kaplan, Alan, Robert Lauriston and Steve Fox. "Groupware," *PC World* (March 1992), pp. 209-214. "No network office can live without electronic mail. Once you discover group scheduling, editing, and contact management, you may not be able to live without groupware, either." The

TECHNOLOGY AND THE FUTURE OF FUNDRAISING

article briefly describes 24 programs now on the market that offer some or all of these features.

Lewis, Peter H. "Report with Sound Effects and Video: Apple Quicktime Takes Desktop Publishing into a New Dimension," *New York Times* (January 12, 1992), p. 8. This recent innovation from Apple "holds the promise of making video, animation and sound almost as easy to use in computer programs as text and graphics." And it's already on the market and in use. "Video clips, stereo sound and animated sequences can be stored on a floppy disk (in small snippets) or hard drive just as text and graphics can be stored — except that video requires much more disk space than plain text or graphics." Similar products are in development for IBM-compatible PCs running Windows.

Maivald, Jim. "Pen Computers Will Rule," *Business Publishing* (January 1992), pp. 12-13. "Advancements in voice-recognition capabilities may very well spell the end of the keyboard and the computer as we know it." And pen-based computers will "change the way people use and think about documents... Although live documents will cost more to produce initially, updates and corrections can be published at a fraction of the cost of paper-based documents."

Markoff, John. "Is the Electronic Book Closer Than You Think?," *New York Times* (December 29, 1991), p. 5. "Publishers are starting to see the allure of selling words without paper or ink... Next year Adobe Inc., the largest maker of software for desktop publishing systems, plans to introduce Carousel, which it hopes will pave the way toward a single format for electronic books. When stored as a Carousel document, a book or magazine could be read on Macintosh and I.B.M.-compatible computers, or on a special book viewer..."

——————. "Adobe Tackles the Paper Glut with a Software for All Systems," *New York Times* (December 22, 1991), p. 9. A preview of Adobe's Carousel system, which "permits users of I.B.M. DOS-compatible, Windows, Apple Macintosh and Unix-based computers to exchange electronic documents that include text, graphics and illustrations." Markoff speculates that this "could have a profound effect on the way computer-based documents are distributed and used."

....

————. "For the PC User, Vast Libraries — And Getting the Data Will Be Simplified," *New York Times* (July 3, 1991), pp. D1, D5. Markoff reports on the makings of "a nationwide computerized library system." "Already, an experimental computer library has linked 150 universities to 40 sources of information, ranging from National Institutes of Health data to corporate documents and Shakespeare's plays. New software allows users to browse or zero in on particular information... Mitchell Kapor... predicts the growth of a new industry as significant as the personal computer business... The Government proposes to expand and improve Internet [now linking scientific researchers worldwide] by financing a National Research and Education Network, or NREN, that could extend high-speed computer links into schools and communities across the country."

Ramirez, Anthony. "The Ultimate Portable-Phone Plan," *New York Times* (March 18, 1992), pp. C1, C6. Motorola Inc.'s proposed Iridium system would employ 77 low-orbiting satellites to achieve genuine world-wide reach for cellular telephones — for an estimated investment of more than $3 billion in hardware. Iridium is foreseen as a network for international business travelers, disaster relief workers, and other heavily-subsidized callers — not the person on the street. The cost: $3,500 for an Iridium telephone set, plus a $50 per month service fee and $15 for a five-minute conversation — plus locally levied long-distance fees.

Reid, T. R. "Computers Without Screens or Keyboards Are on the Horizon," *Washington Post* (date unknown). "Makers can produce PCs with calculator-sized screens, but then they become too tiny to see... The idea is to build a computer that makes its own display screen out of thin air. In other words, the computer projects the display in the air in front of you, something like those alarm clocks that project a digital readout of the time onto the ceiling... Designers are actually working on these devices, some using light-projection systems roughly similar to slide projectors, some using holographic techniques."

Reinhardt, Andy. "Momenta Points to the Future: A New Notebook Merges the Pen, the Keyboard, and a Slick — but Risky — New GUI," *Byte* (November 1991), pp. 48-49. Sporting a distinctive Graphical User Interface

(GUI), Momenta's pen-based laptop computer is aimed at "mobile executives, not at the blue-collar and field workers who have until now been the target audience for pen-based PCs." With 4MB of RAM, a 40-MB hard drive and a built-in fax/data modem, the machine retails for $4995.

Rheingold, Howard. *Virtual Reality: The Revolutionary Technology of Computer-Generated Artificial Worlds — and How It Promises and Threatens to Transform Business and Society.* New York: Summit Books, 1991. Hardcover, 415 pages. The current editor of the *Whole Earth Quarterly*, himself healthily skeptical about the supposed benefits of technology, waxes eloquent about the brilliant future of these quirky new devices that create illusions in the grandest sense and immerse us in worlds otherwise beyond our vision. Rheingold successfully argues, however, that virtual reality has already paid off in very substantial ways in biomedical research. Who knows? The guy may be right: this field, which looks today like a byway on the larger map of emerging technology, could prove to be the main route to the future!

Schwartz, Evan I., and James B. Treece. "Smart Programs Go to Work: How Applied-Intelligence Software Makes Decisions for the Real World," *Business Week* (March 2, 1992), pp. 96-105. "Applied intelligence — software that 'knows,' rather than software that 'thinks'" — is playing an ever more prominent role in industry and government alike. The "knowledge of how manufactured goods are built and how they work makes up 70% of their development costs. And in service businesses, such as selling mutual funds, that percentage is about 90%."

Taylor, David A., Ph.D. *Object-Oriented Technology: A Manager's Guide.* Reading, Massachusetts: Addison-Wesley Publishing Company, Inc., 1990. Softcover, 147 pages.

Trefil, James. "A Picture Is Worth a Zillion Bits," *New York Times Book Review* (March 15, 1992), p. 20. Trefil writes that Stephen S. Hall's new book, *Mapping the Next Millennium: The Discovery of New Geographies*, advances the interesting thesis that "virtually all modern scientific research can be seen as a process for making maps." This "produces maps of the brain, of chaotic systems, of the far reaches of the solar system, of the universe itself. Why is this such an important insight? Because, as the

....

world overwhelms us with data — "factoids," if you will — we must turn to comprehensible visual representations, or maps, to make sense of it all. And, as the years go by, Trefil argues, "the visual display of information will become increasingly important."

Venditto, Gus. "Intel Readies Key Tools for Integrating DVI with MPC," *PC Magazine* (December 31, 1991), p. 29. In 1992, Intel will introduce an $1,895 computer board featuring DVI (Digital Video Interactive) capacity that will permit users to manipulate and view video on a PC, along with a $695 add-on board "that lets you capture video from a camcorder or VCR."

Weinberger, David D. "The Active Document: Making Pages Smarter," *The Futurist* (July-August 1991), pp. 25-28. "Future documents will think and act for themselves, adding [and updating] information, changing graphics, and even determining what readers may or may not see."

Workplace Giving Campaign Holds Lessons for the Future

In the late summer and fall of 1992, I worked with one of the world's leading high-tech manufacturers and merchants — Apple Computer, Inc. — to overhaul their workplace giving campaign. The resulting effort raised over 60 percent more money than the campaign had brought in the preceding year — and more than doubled the number of participating employees. It was a fascinating experience and motivated me to write a detailed article for Fund Raising Management magazine. (The article appeared in July 1993; I'll send you a copy, if you wish.)

Most of my work for Apple consisted of transforming a campaign based on the company's traditional image and identity advertising techniques — "mass advertising," if you will — into targeted, personalized, one-on-one communications modeled on classic direct mail fundraising techniques. The lion's share of our effort involved sending letters from Fred Silverman, the Apple executive in charge of the program, to thousands of individual Apple employees.

There was a lot of collateral advertising as well. The poster reproduced on the opposite page was the third of a series of three posted at two-week intervals during the six weeks of the campaign. We used the Apple employee newsletter, too.

IT'S YOUR TURN NOW.

Jennie Tsunekawa, Carmen Segovia, Peter Trump, Mary Fordham, Peter Parkinson, Mark Manley, Rosa Radicchi, Marilyn Roach, Jonathan Peon, Barbara Andersen, Sharon Hale, Suki Lee, Katie Adler, Carol Foote, Mike Williams, Michael Teener, Judy Specht, Stan Karp, Jordan Hickey, Mary Mangone, Sarah Parks, Jimmy Melton, all donors to the 1993 Apple Employee Giving Campaign.

Make the choice.
Pledge your support to help those in need.
We did.

Return your pledge form by Thursday, Oct. 22

1993 Apple Employee Giving Campaign

THINK GLOBALLY. GIVE LOCALLY.

Yes, I want to make the choice.

☐ Tell me more.
Just return this card, or call (408) 974-7825 for more information on the 1993 Apple Employee Giving Campaign, and how you can make the choice.

Name _____
Mailstop _____
Apple Phone # _____

A program of Apple Community Affairs

♻ recyclable and made from recycled paper

 THINK GLOBALLY. GIVE LOCALLY.

....

But the most intriguing collateral effort was — no surprise here — to use Apple employees' computers. How we did so holds lessons for the use of E-mail in other, future fundraising efforts.

Naturally, we turned to the computer for its ability to store and sort information. Without database management capabilities, we could never have personalized all those letters. But there were two more interesting ways we tapped the computer's power:

1. For most of Apple's 6,000 San Francisco Bay Area employees, their first glimpse of the 1993 Apple Employee Giving Campaign was the following message. That image appeared on their computer screens on Tuesday, Oct. 6, when they logged onto the company's electronic mail (E-mail) system.

 AppleLink   Extra

Tuesday	October 6, 1992

5*NEWS: Oct. 6 '92 Editorial Lineup

How does MacWEEK get the scoop on Apple? Read all about it in a 5*NEWS interview with editor-in-chief Dan Farber on pg. 3. On pg. 1, Apple pubs group saves millions and Sculley outlines a most colorful future. Pg 4? Employee/Exec Foru m wrapup. Check it out in the Oct. 6 issue, coming to you today!

> See: (HotLinks:) Apple Community News: 5*NEWS

Think Globally. Give Locally.

You can do something about the world's problems. Pledge your support today to one of more than 200 groups working to meet human or environmental needs.

The **1993 Apple Employee Giving Campaign** runs October 6 - 22. Questions? Call the Apple Employee Giving Hotline at (408) 974-7825.

> See: (Employees:) HotLinks: Apple Community News: Apple Employee Giving Campaign

TECHNOLOGY AND THE FUTURE OF FUNDRAISING

Follow-up screens appeared on Oct. 16 and on Oct. 20, two days before the campaign's formal last day. Thus E-mail became a form of collateral advertising, cueing employees to information available through other communications media — and giving them a ready way to respond by indicating interest or asking a question directly through their computers.

2. More importantly, Apple posted on the E-mail system its full database of information about the more than 500 charities participating in the campaign. Apple employees could browse directly through that database, avoiding paper altogether. We also made that information available on paper ("hardcopy" to computer nuts), and we printed shorter versions of it in several places, including a centerfold insert in the employee newsletter.

I believe both these uses of computer technology presage the interactive fundraising efforts of the future. What will be different then, however, is that many, if not all, of our donors will be reachable through such means. And we'll continue seeking them out through other means as well. The new technologies won't entirely supplant the old: at first, they'll supplement the more traditional forms of communication; then, gradually, they'll assume a more and more dominant role, but techniques such as good, old-fashioned direct mail will be around for a long time to come.

That's the way I see it. How about you?

TECHNOLOGY AND THE FUTURE OF FUNDRAISING

· ·

*Now's a good time to check out the questionnaire I tucked
into that brightly colored envelope at the front of this book.
Thanks for sticking with me for the distance!*

TECHNOLOGY AND THE FUTURE OF FUNDRAISING

GLOSSARY

Batch processing — A system of updating donor files or other lists in batches. Normally, this requires separate data entry staff and entails some delay following the receipt of a gift or other information requiring the update.

CD-ROM — Engineers have tried an amazing variety of means to store and deliver information on computers, and some have never caught on; even the most popular are eventually dropped in favor of superior technology. Early computers commonly used paper tape. Then came magnetic tape, followed by floppy disks and so-called hard disk drives (which are rarely hard enough to make me feel safe). Now there's "CD-ROM," which is similar to — but, naturally, incompatible with — the Compact Disks that play music. The jury's out on CD-ROM, one of the more ambitious latter-day efforts to establish a universal standard: the manufacturers of different brands of CD-ROM players are fighting now, a lot like the proponents of VHS and Beta-format videotape recorders once did.

Cheshire label — Those flimsy white paper mailing labels that are affixed to so many direct mail appeals. They're usually printed 44 labels per page on large sheets of computer paper.

Computer modeling — A product of collaboration between statisticians and computer jockeys. The statistician claims to be able to predict the likelihood of future behavior based on evidence of past behavior. The computer jock claims to be able to mimic real-life experience by ranking and combining all measurable statistical predictors of behavior in a computer program. Typically, a

....

"computer model" assigns a number (say, 4.6 on a scale of 1 to 10) that will predict the chances that an individual donor will respond favorably to a specific appeal. In real life, this stuff doesn't always work, of course.

Data cards — File cards produced by list brokers that contain basic information about the lists they're hawking.

Desktop publishing — These days, typically one of a handful of software products that enable a ham-fisted klutz like the author to produce finished, camera-ready artwork of passable quality — including both text and graphic images — with an inexpensive desktop computer and laser printer.

Electronic Funds Transfer — A way for your organization to cut fundraising costs and virtually eliminate checks and other paperwork by receiving gifts from donors through direct transfer, bank to bank. This isn't as big a deal as you might think. For starters, money is not that stuff you've got in your wallet; the world just doesn't work that way anymore. Most of our country's money exists in the form of electronic impulses floating in the ozone. Your checking account, for example, consists of a set of digitized numbers recorded on a computer somewhere — and those numbers probably change on a daily basis. What's the big deal, then, for donors to authorize the transfer of money from their checking accounts directly to the accounts of their favorite charities — when all that's really happening is that a few electronic impulses are sent from one bank's computer to another's? Perhaps those donors haven't caught on yet. I hope you do.

Expert system — A sophisticated type of software used most widely in manufacturing companies but now beginning to find its way into the direct marketing industry. In an "expert system," the accumulated experience of a genuine human expert in a specialized field is codified in a computer program. Less experienced people trained to ask questions of the computer can, supposedly, obtain answers to even the most complex technical questions that fully reflect the expert's views — and are available almost instantaneously.

Geodemographics — The art (some foolishly say science) of targeting direct mail recipients based on geography and the interests, abilities or attitudes believed to be associated with specific neighborhoods. For example, some might assume a homeowner living in an "upscale" ZIP code is a good donor prospect. But little do they know!

Groupware — An imprecise term that usually means a general type of software which enables groups of people to work together simultaneously on text, artwork, spreadsheets or other computer files.

IVR — If there's any industry more addicted to acronyms than the computer industry, it's telemarketing. "IVR" stands for "Interactive Voice Response," but between you and me what it really means is voice-mail. However, IVR is a special, high-volume form of voice-mail that's now often used in answering 800- and 900-numbers. For the most part, it seems to be a technique to avoid employing human operators. The only thing "interactive" about IVR is that a caller is sometimes offered the option of leaving a voice recording, punching in numbers on a telephone keypad — and listening to one or another rubber-voiced recordings depending upon whether she presses "1" or "3."

LAN — "Local Area Network." A bunch of computers linked together, usually by wires, so they may share information. Unlike a

....

WAN ("Wide Area Network"), a LAN is typically located at a single site.

Linotronic — That smooth, shiny white printout the type-setter sends to the designer for paste-up or directly to the printer.

Match-fill — Personalized information (such as a donor's name or giving data) that is inserted into a blank position in pre-printed text, often using a typeface chosen to match that of the text.

Multimedia — If you want to watch computer freaks freak out, just ask them to agree on a definition of "multimedia." Commonly, this term refers to the stuff you can do with a computer that is equipped with CD-ROM drive and other special attachments, including a "sound board" that enables the machine to make the most amazingly obscene noises. But don't expect a computer expert to agree with that definition.

Multivariate analysis — Pick this fancy phrase apart, and you'll get the point: this is a form of statistical analysis that attempts to take a large number of variable factors into account and generally requires a fast computer.

Neural network — Computers don't think like humans, at least not yet — but software like this might make you think they can. In a "neural network" — a simple form of what is inelegantly called "artificial intelligence" — the programmer attempts to mimic the way humans learn from experience and weigh independent variables to make decisions. Some psychologists define intelligence as an ability to recognize patterns — and that's what neural networks do, often better, and almost always far faster, than humans. If computers scare you, just wait until they get really good at writing this stuff!

On-line database management — Unlike "batch processing," an on-line system allows a charity or its computer service bureau to update a donor file at the same time as an individual gift is being recorded in the caging and cashiering process.

On-line web press — A very large, costly, high-speed press that prints (often in full color) on enormous rolls of paper; cuts, folds and sometimes staples the paper into individual mailing pieces; imprints individual recipients' names and addresses, usually in far too many places; and delivers the finished product, bundled in ZIP code (or even carrier route) order, ready for the letter-carrier's tender ministrations.

On-line conferencing — I made this one up. Today, businesses — and, occasionally, nonprofits — are making more and more use of video teleconferencing; prices on teleconferencing equipment have come down to the point that even some small businesses are buying or leasing the stuff rather than trucking their staff members or clients off to special rented facilities. It's already possible to do a limited amount of video teleconferencing on a "LAN" or "WAN" using some forms of "groupware." I'm betting the time isn't far off when E-mail will commonly include both sound and video recordings as well as text — and be usable in "real time" (computer jargon for "right now.")

Outbound and inbound phone — Out-going calls (usually solicitations) and in-coming calls (normally using toll-free 800-numbers) usually require different procedures and different staff. Many telephone service bureaus specialize in one field or the other, but not both.

....

Psychographics — A ten-dollar word for the attitudes and lifestyle characteristics that targeting experts associate with certain lists.

Selective binding and inserting — An extension of the concept of the "on-line web press" now increasingly used in the magazine industry. Ridiculously expensive equipment is used to compile sometimes radically different editions of a magazine, choosing stories and ads for one edition and rejecting them for another — all in the same continuous, computer-mediated printing process.

Spreadsheet— Refers to both a type of software and its product, which is usually a page-full of barely legible numbers arrayed in innumerable columns and rows labeled with obscure (and often indecipherable) abbreviations.

WAN — A "Wide Area Network," common only in large corporations and other multi-site institutions, is a way to join together large numbers of computers that are widely dispersed. (See also "LAN.") Generally, the computer industry has moved away from designing systems that require guys in white coats to run them — but this is a development that goes in the opposite direction. If you don't believe me, just try reading a news article about this subject in a computer trade journal! (You'll probably find it in the section labeled "enterprise management," which gives you some idea what's going on.)

ZIP+4+4 — Thirty years ago we got the five-digit ZIP code. Now, they're trying to talk us into adding four more digits (and some of us are even doing it, because it usually pays to do so). But just wait: in no time flat, your ZIP code will be longer than your Social Security number!

ABOUT THE AUTHOR

I'm the founder and chairman of Mal Warwick & Associates Inc. (Berkeley, California), specializing in direct mail fundraising, and co-founder and chairman of a telephone fundraising firm, The Progressive Group Inc. (Hadley, Massachusetts). Together with my colleagues in the two companies, I've raised well over $100 million for nonprofit organizations and political committees since 1979. My clients have included hundreds of charitable causes and institutions as well as five leading Democratic Presidential candidates.

Since 1990, I've been writing a monthly column ("The Warwick File") for *The NonProfit Times*. I edit and publish a newsletter (*Successful Direct Mail & Telephone Fundraising*™) and am the author of three previous books the most recent of which was *999 Tips, Trends and Guidelines for Successful Direct Mail & Telephone Fundraising*, (Strathmoor Press, 1993). Another book, *How to Write Successful Fundraising Letters*, will be published in March 1994. I also speak frequently at conferences and workshops all over the U.S. and Canada.

....

I'm active in the National Society of Fund Raising Executives (NSFRE) and serve as President of the Association of Direct Response Fundraising Counsel (ADRFCO), the national trade association of direct mail fundraising consultants.

I was a Peace Corps Volunteer (Ecuador, 1965-69) and still spend a good deal of my time on volunteer activities. The nonprofits that take most of my time these days are the Berkeley Community Fund, which I co-founded and serve as chair of the Executive Committee, and the Berkeley Symphony Orchestra, where I'm the Vice President of the board. I'm also a director of Bay Area Renewal, the Pacific Institute for Studies in Environment, Development and Security and the Jewish Film Festival. I was a founding member of Business for Social Responsibility and sat on its national board and executive committee during its first year, just now ending.

HOW THIS BOOK WAS BIRTHED

T echnology and the Future of Fundraising was conceived, drafted, edited, designed, laid out and "outputted" on a simple, garden-variety IBM-compatible personal computer sitting on my desk at home. As the author, I enjoyed nearly total control over every detail of the book's production, so I'm to blame for any errors you find. I'm also immodestly proud of the effort and will do my best to be gracious if you find something in the book to praise.

Although three months elapsed from conception to delivery of the first printed copies of this book, the first draft — circulated to my peers for comment — required all of 32 hours to produce. If that fact makes you gasp, check out the Introduction, where you'll learn that nearly all the contents of this book were adapted from materials I'd written for workshops and lectures. So I didn't actually *write* this

....

work in 32 hours. In fact, it required about three years. And, truth to tell, I invested considerable time drafting additional material as well as editing what I'd already done -- *after* digesting the comments I received about the first draft.

The hardware I used was unexceptional by the technological standards of 1993: an Intel 486 DX microprocessor running at 33-megahertz, a Radius Pivot 17-inch full-page color monitor and a Hewlett-Packard LaserJet III equipped with a LaserMaster Postscript thingamajig that my computer consultants have never completely made me understand. (All I know is, the thing allows my HP III to print both text and graphics at 800 x 800 dots-per-inch, which is, as you may be aware, not such a big deal these days.)

The software I used was just as pedestrian as the hardware. I drafted the text and formatted the manuscript in WordPerfect 5.2 for Windows, then (early adopter that I am) edited the copy in version 6.0. Later, I stripped out the WordPerfect formatting codes and imported the text into Ventura Publisher 4.1, my clunky but functional desktop publishing program. Ventura allowed me to do the fancy stuff: repeating frames, page headers and footers, and all those nifty fonts ("typefaces" to the uninitiated). I swore a lot during the process, but, truth to tell, I had a ball. I hope that's reflected in the book you hold in your hands.

So, that's how this book was born. But now it's up to you. Because this book hasn't truly begun to live until you read it!

— M.W.

Order These Publications By Mal Warwick

> **999 Tips, Trends and Guidelines for Successful Direct Mail and Telephone Fundraising**, softcover, indexed, 316 pp. (1993), $34.95 (plus $2.88 sales tax in California).

> **Revolution in the Mailbox**: How Direct Mail Fundraising Is Changing the Face of American Society — And How Your Organization Can Benefit, hardcover, indexed and profusely illustrated, 312 pp. (1990), $29.95 (plus $2.47 sales tax in California).

> **Successful Direct Mail & Telephone Fundraising**™— 12 pages, quarterly. Every issue includes What's Working (& What's Not), Tips & Timesavers, The Copy Corner, The Q&A Department, a featured package, examples galore. Subscription: $49.95 for 1 year. For more information, call toll-free 1-800-217-7377.

> **You Don't Always Get What You Ask For: Using Direct Mail Tests to Raise More Money for Your Organization,** softcover, 126 pp. (1992), $19.95 (plus $1.65 sales tax per copy for California residents).

TITLE	QUAN	@	TOTAL
999 Tips, Trends and Guidelines		$34.95	
Revolution in the Mailbox		29.95	
Successful Direct Mail & Telephone Fundraising (1 year subscription)		49.95	
You Don't Always Get What You Ask For		19.95	
Subtotal			
Californians: add 8.25% sales tax			
Shipping/handling (per item)		3.00	
TOTAL			

SHIPPING INFORMATION	
Name	
Title	
Organization	
Address	
Address	
City/State/ZIP	
Phone	( )

COPY OR CLIP THIS PAGE and mail with your check payable to "STRATHMOOR PRESS" to: Strathmoor Press, Order Fulfillment Center, 2550 Ninth Street, Suite 1040, Berkeley, CA 94710-2516

ORDERS ARE NORMALLY SHIPPED the week they're received, but please allow 4-6 weeks for delivery. Call (800) 217-7377 for information about express shipping options.

CREDIT CARD ORDERS: phone toll-free (800) 217-7377 or fax (510) 843-0142.